Many Voices
TWO BOOKS IN ONE
BOOK I

Many Voices

A Collection of Poems
Suitable for Choral Speech

Made by
MONA SWANN

TWO BOOKS IN ONE
BOOK I

Granger Index Reprint Series

BOOKS FOR LIBRARIES PRESS
FREEPORT, NEW YORK

First Published 1934
Reprinted 1971

INTERNATIONAL STANDARD BOOK NUMBER:
0-8369-6248-6

LIBRARY OF CONGRESS CATALOG CARD NUMBER:
72-149166

PRINTED IN THE UNITED STATES OF AMERICA

PREFACE

MANY VOICES is a collection of poems whose impersonality of outlook allows them to be spoken aloud chorally. In Book I the poems are graded for choirs of boys and girls from the age of eight to about twelve; in Book II they are arranged chronologically, and are suited to older choirs of all ages according to their several capacities.

In order to avoid to some extent one of the great drawbacks of anthologies—that of duplication—no poems are included in Book I, and only four in Book II, which are in Palgrave's *Golden Treasury* (Macmillan edition). For this reason several excellent choral poems are omitted; a list of these, however, is given in *An Approach to Choral Speech*.[1] There too will be found suggestions for the training of choirs and for the use of these anthologies, with indications of the varied types of choral speaking that different poems demand—unison, antiphonal, group, cumulative, solo with choral refrain, etc.

MONA SWANN

Moira House
  Eastbourne

---

[1]*An Approach to Choral Speech* by Mona Swann.

INDEX OF AUTHORS

BOOK I

INDEX OF TITLES AND FIRST LINES

BOOK I

Titles—*Italics*   First Lines—Roman

viii

INDEX OF TITLES AND FIRST LINES

INDEX OF TITLES AND FIRST LINES

KINGS AND QUEENS

EIGHT Henries, one Mary,
  One Elizabeth;
Crowned and throned Kings and Queens
  Now lie still in death.

Four Williams, one Stephen,
  Anne, Victoria, John:
Sceptre and orb are laid aside;
  All are to quiet gone.
And James and Charles, and Charles's sons—
  They, too, have journeyed on.

Three Richards, seven Edwards
  Their royal hour did thrive;
They sleep with Georges one to four:
  And we praise God for five.

                  Walter de la Mare

THE KEY OF THE KINGDOM

THIS is the Key of the Kingdom:

In that Kingdom there is a city;
In that city there is a town;
In that town there is a street;

In that street there is a lane;
In that lane there is a yard;
In that yard there is a house;
In that house there is a room;
In that room there is a bed;
On that bed there is a basket;
And in that basket there are sweet flowers.

Flowers in the basket,
Basket on the bed,
Bed in the room,
Room in the house,
House in the yard,
Yard in the lane,
Lane in the street,
Street in the town,
Town in the city,
City in the Kingdom:
   This is the Key of the Kingdom!

Traditional

SEASONS

OH the cheerful Budding-time!
   When thorn-hedges turn to green,
When new leaves of elm and lime
   Cleave and shed their winter screen;
Tender lambs are born and baa,
   North wind finds no snow to bring,
Vigorous Nature laughs "Ha ha!"
   In the miracle of Spring.

Oh the gorgeous Blossom-days!
   When broad flag-flowers drink and blow:
In and out in Summer-blaze
   Dragon-flies flash to and fro;
Ashen branches hang out keys;
   Oaks put forth the rosy shoot,
Wandering herds wax sleek at ease,
   Lovely blossoms end in fruit.

Oh the shouting Harvest-weeks!
   Mother Earth grows fat with sheaves;
Thrifty gleaner finds who seeks;
   Russet-golden pomp of leaves
Crowns the woods, to fall at length;
   Bracing winds are felt to stir,
Ocean gathers up her strength,
   Beasts renew their dwindled fur.

Oh the starving Winter lapse!
   Ice-bound, hunger-pinched, and dim!
Dormant roots recall their saps,
   Empty nests show black and grim.
Short-lived sunshine gives no heat,
   Undue buds are nipped by frost,
Snow sets forth a winding-sheet,
   And all hope of life seems lost.

Christina Rossetti

OXFORDSHIRE MAY-SONG

SPRING is coming, spring is coming;
   Birdies, build your nest!
Weave together straw and feather,
   Doing each your best.

Spring is coming, spring is coming,
  Flowers are coming too;
Pansies, lilies, daffodillies,
  Now are coming through.

Spring is coming, spring is coming,
  All around is fair;
Shimmer and quiver on the river,
  Joy is everywhere!

We wish you a happy May!

Anon.

FIRST SPRING MORNING

LOOK! Look! the spring is come:
  O feel the gentle air,
That wanders thro' the boughs to burst
  The thick buds everywhere!
  The birds are glad to see
  The high unclouded sun:
Winter is fled away, they sing,
  The gay time is begun.

  Adown the meadows green
  Let us go dance and play,
And look for violets in the lane,
  And ramble far away
  To gather primroses,
  That in the woodland grow,
And hunt for oxlips, or if yet
  The blades of bluebells show:

4

There the old woodman gruff
Hath half the coppice cut,
And weaves the hurdles all day long
Beside his willow hut.
We'll steal on him, and then
Startle him, all with glee
Singing our song of winter fled
And summer soon to be.

Robert Bridges

SONG OF THE BLUEBELLS

SWEET bluebells we,
Mid flowers of the lea,
The likest in hue to heaven,
Our bonnets so blue
Are tinged with the dew
That drops from the sky at even.

Our bloom more sweet
Than dark violet,
Or tulip's purple stain,
At every return
Of the dew-breathing morn,
Grows brighter and brighter again.

George Darley

SPRING

SOUND the flute!
Now it's mute.
Birds delight
Day and night;

Nightingale
In the dale,
Lark in the sky,
Merrily,
Merrily, merrily, to welcome in the year.

Little boy,
Full of joy;
Little girl,
Sweet and small;
Cock does crow,
So do you;
Merry voice,
Infant noise,
Merrily, merrily, to welcome in the year.

Little lamb,
Here I am;
Come and lick
My white neck;
Let me pull
Your soft wool;
Let me kiss
Your soft face:
Merrily, merrily, we welcome in the year.

William Blake

ORCHARD WASSAIL

HERE'S to thee,
Old apple-tree!
Stand fast root,
Bear well top,
Pray God send us
A youling crop!

Every twig
Apple big;
Every bough
Apple enow;
Hats full, caps full,
Fill quarter sacks full!
Holla, boys, holla!
Huzza!

Traditional

GREEN GRASS

A DIS, a dis, a green grass,
A dis, a dis, a dis;
Come all you pretty fair maids
And dance along with us.

For we are going a-roving,
A-roving in this land;
We'll take this pretty fair maid,
We'll take her by the hand.

Ye shall get a duke, my dear,
Ye shall get a drake;
And ye shall get a young prince,
A young prince for your sake.

And if this young prince chance to die,
Ye shall get another;
The bells will ring, and the birds will sing,
And we'll clap hands together.

Traditional

THE SHORT COURTSHIP:
OR THE LUSTY WOOER

HERE comes a lusty wooer,
  My a dildin, my a daldin;
Here comes a lusty wooer,
  Lily bright and shine a'.

Pray who do you woo?
  My a dildin, my a daldin;
Pray who do you woo?
  Lily bright and shine a'.

For your fairest daughter,
  My a dildin, my a daldin;
For your fairest daughter,
  Lily bright and shine a'.

Then there is she for you,
  My a dildin, my a daldin,
Then there is she for you,
  Lily bright and shine a'.

from GAMMER GURTON'S GARLAND   *Traditional*

LAUGHING SONG

WHEN the green woods laugh with the voice of joy,
  And the dimpling stream runs laughing by;
When the air does laugh with our merry wit,
And the green hill laughs with the noise of it;
8

When the meadows laugh with lively green,
And the grasshopper laughs in the merry scene,
When Mary and Susan and Emily
With their sweet round mouths sing "Ha, Ha, He!"

When the painted birds laugh in the shade,
Where our table with cherries and nuts is spread,
Come live, and be merry, and join with me,
To sing the sweet chorus of "Ha, Ha, He!"

William Blake

From *MILL-SONG*

MERRILY the mill-sail
 Turneth round and round,
With a breezy motion
 And a busy sound.
Merrily the miller
 Standeth at the door,
Humming pleasant ditties
 From his ancient store.
Merrily, oh merrily, all the summer's day,
Hums that burly miller, while the mill-sails play.

At the open lattice,
 In the little homestead near
Sits the miller's good wife,
 With face of blythsome cheer;
And round about the gateway
 A little sturdy throng
Of rosy knaves are sporting,
 With laughter loud and strong;
And merrily, right merrily, at close of summer's day,
Aye laugh the miller's children the while the mill-sails
 play. . . .

Thomas Westwood

From *BIRDS IN SUMMER*

HOW pleasant the life of a bird must be,
Flitting about in each leafy tree;
In the leafy trees, so broad and tall,
Like a green and beautiful palace-hall,
With its airy chambers, light and boon,
That open to sun, and stars, and moon;
That open unto the bright blue sky,
And the frolicsome winds as they wander by! . . .

How pleasant the life of a bird must be,
Skimming about on the breezy sea,
Cresting the billows like silvery foam,
Then wheeling away to its cliff-built home!
What joy it must be to sail, upborne
By a strong, free wing, through the rosy morn;
To meet the young sun face to face,
And pierce like a shaft the boundless space:

To pass through the bowers of the silver cloud;
To sing in the thunder-halls aloud;
To spread out the wings for a wild, free flight
With the upper cloud-winds,—oh, what delight!
Oh, what would I give, like a bird, to go
Right on through the arch of the sun-lit bow,
And see how the water-drops are kissed
Into green and yellow and amethyst! . . .

What joy it must be, like a living breeze,
To flutter about 'mid the flowering trees;
Lightly to soar, and see beneath
The wastes of the blossoming purple heath,

10

And the yellow furze, like fields of gold
That gladdened some fairy region old!
On mountain-tops, on the billowy sea,
On the leafy stems of the forest-tree,
How pleasant the life of a bird must be!

Mary Howitt

From *BIRDS' FOOD*

LONG-LEGS, hasten away!
  Cockchafers, leave your play!
The searching Rook for you doth look
  Throughout the livelong day.

Snail with wreathèd shell,
  Slugs of grove and dell,
The parent Thrush on you will rush,
  And bear you off to his cell. . . .

Dragon-flies brightly blue!
  King-fisher hawks for you;
See, over the stream, like a rainbow gleam,
  She's hovering now in view. . . .

Glow-worms, hide your light;
  The warbling Bird of Night
On you will sup! he'll gobble you up;
  You'd better not shine too bright. . . .

Hop away, croaking frog,
  The Bittern is come to the bog;
The bittern that booms in the evening glooms,
  As loud as the baying dog.

Sara Coleridge

THE LARK'S GRAVE

WE'LL plant a cornflower on his grave,
  And a grain of the bearded barley,
And a little bluebell to ring his knell,
  And eyebright, blossoming early;
    And we'll cover it over
    With purple clover,
  And daisies, crimson and pearly.

And we'll pray the Linnet to chant his dirge,
  With the Robin and Wren for chorus;
His mate, on high, shall rain from the sky
  Her benedictus o'er us,
    And the Hawks and Owls,
    Those pitiless fowls,
  We'll drive away before us.

And then we'll leave him to his rest,
  And whisper soft above him,
That ever his song was sweet and strong,
  Nor cloud nor mist could move him;
    In his strain was a gladness
    To cure all sadness,
  And all fair things did love him.

Thomas Westwood

ROBIN REDBREAST

GOOD-BYE, good-bye to Summer!
  For Summer's nearly done;
The garden smiling faintly,
  Cool breezes in the sun;
Our thrushes now are silent,
  Our swallows flown away,—

But Robin's here in coat of brown,
   With ruddy breast-knot gay.
     Robin, Robin Redbreast,
     O Robin dear!
     Robin singing sweetly
      In the falling year.

Bright yellow, red, and orange,
   The leaves come down in hosts;
The trees are Indian Princes,
   But soon they'll turn to Ghosts;
The scanty pears and apples
   Hang russet on the bough;
It's Autumn, Autumn, Autumn late,
   'Twill soon be Winter now.
     Robin, Robin Redbreast,
     O Robin dear!
     And welaway! my Robin,
      For pinching times are near.

The fireside for the Cricket,
   The wheatstack for the Mouse,
When trembling night-winds whistle
   And moan all round the house;
The frosty ways like iron,
   The branches plumed with snow,—
Alas, in Winter, dead and dark,
   Where can poor Robin go?
     Robin, Robin Redbreast,
     O Robin dear!
     And a crumb of bread for Robin,
      His little heart to cheer.
          William Allingham

MY COCK LILY-COCK

I HAD a cock and a cock loved me,
    And I fed my cock under a hollow tree:
  My cock cried—Cock, cock, coo!
Everybody loves their cock, and I love my cock too!

I had a hen, and a hen loved me,
And I fed my hen under a hollow tree:
  My hen went Chickle-chackle, chickle-chackle!
  My cock cried—Cock, cock, coo!
Everybody loves their cock, and I love my cock too!

I had a goose, and a goose loved me,
And I fed my goose under a hollow tree:
  My goose went—Qu'k, qu'k, qu'k!
  My hen, etc.

I had a duck, and a duck loved me,
And I fed my duck under a hollow tree:
  My duck went—Quack, quack, quack!
  My goose, etc.

I had a drake, and a drake loved me,
And I fed my drake under a hollow tree:
  My drake went—Ca-qua, ca-qua, ca-qua!
  My duck, etc.

I had a cat, and a cat loved me,
And I fed my cat under a hollow tree:
  My cat went—Miaow, miaow, miaow!
  My drake, etc.

I had a dog, and a dog loved me,
And I fed my dog under a hollow tree:
  My dog went—Bow, wow, wow!
  My cat, etc.

I had a cow, and a cow loved me,
And I fed my cow under a hollow tree:
   My cow went—Moo, moo, moo!
   My dog, etc.

I had a sheep, and a sheep loved me,
And I fed my sheep under a hollow tree:
   My sheep went—Baa, baa, baa!
   My cow, etc.

I had a donkey, and a donkey loved me,
And I fed my donkey under a hollow tree:
   My donkey went—Hee-haw, hee-haw!
   My sheep, etc.

I had a horse, and a horse loved me,
And I fed my horse under a hollow tree:
   My horse went—Whin-neigh-h-h-h-h!
   My donkey, etc.

I had a pig, and a pig loved me,
And I fed my pig under a hollow tree:
   My pig went—Hoogh, hoogh, hoogh!
   My horse went—Whin-neigh-h-h-h-h!
   My donkey went—Hee-haw, hee-haw!
   My sheep went—Baa, baa, baa!
   My cow went—Moo, moo, moo!
   My dog went—Bow, wow, wow!
   My cat went—Miaow, miaow, miaow!
   My drake went—Ca-qua, ca-qua, ca-qua!
   My duck went—Quack, quack, quack!
   My goose went—Qu'k, qu'k, qu'k!
   My hen went—Chickle-chackle, chickle-chackle!
   My cock cried—Cock, cock, coo!
Everybody loves their cock, and I love my cock too!
Traditional

A DIRGE FOR A RIGHTEOUS KITTEN

(To be intoned, all but the two italicized lines, which are to
be spoken in a snappy, matter-of-fact way)

DING-DONG, ding-dong, ding-dong.
 Here lies a kitten good, who kept
A kitten's proper place.
He stole no pantry eatables,
Nor scratched the baby's face.
He let the alley-cats alone.
He had no yowling vice.
His shirt was always laundried well,
He freed the house of mice.
Until his death he had not caused
His little mistress tears,
He wore his ribbon prettily,
He washed behind his ears.
Ding-dong, ding-dong, ding-dong.

        Vachel Lindsay

THE BARLEY-MOWERS' SONG

BARLEY-MOWERS here we stand,
 One, two, three, a steady band;
True of heart and strong of limb,
Ready in our harvest-trim;
All a-row, with spirits blithe,
Now we whet the bended scythe.
 Rink-a-tink, rink-a-tink, rink-a-tink-a-tink!

16

Side by side now, bending low,
Down the swaths of barley go;
Stroke by stroke, as true as chime
Of the bells, we keep in time:
Then we whet the ringing scythe,
Standing 'mid the barley lithe.
   Rink-a-tink, rink-a-tink, rink-a-tink-a-tink! . . .

. . . Day and night, and night and day,
Time, the mower, will not stay:
We may hear him in our path
By the falling barley-swath;
While we sing with spirits blithe,
We may hear his ringing scythe.
   Rink-a-tink, rink-a-tink, rink-a-tink-a-tink!
                                        Mary Howitt

CHURNING CHARM

(To be said thrice)

COME, butter, come;
   Come, butter, come;
Peter stands at the gate
Waiting for a buttered cake,
   Come, butter, come;
   Come, butter, come.
                              Traditional

THE LAST WILL AND TESTAMENT
OF THE GREY MARE

JOHN COOK he had a little grey mare;
  He, haw, hum!
Her back stood up, and her bones they were bare;
  He, haw, hum!

John Cook was riding up Shuters Bank;
  He, haw, hum!
And there his nag did kick and prank;
  He, haw, hum!

John Cook was riding up Shuters Hill;
  He, haw hum!
His mare fell down and she made her will;
  He, haw, hum!

The saddle and bridle were laid on the shelf;
  He, haw, hum!
If you want any more you may sing it yourself!
  He, haw, hum!

                  Traditional

WASHING-DAY

THEY that wash on Monday
  Have all the week to dry;
They that wash on Tuesday
  Are not much awry;
They that wash on Wednesday
  Are not much to blame;

They that wash on Thursday,
   Wash for shame;
They that wash on Friday,
   Wash in need;
They that wash on Saturday,
   Oh! they're sluts indeed!

from GAMMER GURTON'S GARLAND   *Traditional*

FAREWELL TO THE FARM

THE coach is at the door at last!
  The eager children, mounting fast
And kissing hands, in chorus sing:
Good-bye, good-bye, to everything!

To house and garden, field and lawn,
The meadow-gates we swang upon,
To pump and stable, tree and swing,
Good-bye, good-bye to everything!

And fare you well for ever more,
O ladder at the hayloft door,
O hayloft where the cobwebs cling,
Good-bye, good-bye, to everything!

Crack goes the whip, and off we go;
The trees and houses smaller grow;
Last, round the woody turn we swing:
Good-bye, good-bye, to everything!
            Robert Louis Stevenson

19

FROM A RAILWAY CARRIAGE

FASTER than fairies, faster than witches,
  Bridges and houses, hedges and ditches;
And charging along like troops in a battle,
All through the meadows the horses and cattle:
All of the sights of the hill and the plain
Fly as thick as driving rain;
And ever again, in the wink of an eye,
Painted stations whistle by.

Here is a child who clambers and scrambles,
All by himself, and gathering brambles;
Here is a tramp who stands and gazes;
And there is the green for stringing the daisies!
Here is a cart run away in the road
Lumping along with man and load;
And here is a mill and there is a river:
Each a glimpse and gone for ever!

Robert Louis Stevenson

A CHILL

WHAT can lambkins do
    All the keen night through?
Nestle by their woolly mother,
  The careful ewe.

  What can nestlings do
  In the nightly dew?
Sleep beneath their mother's wing
  Till day break anew.

If in field or tree
There might only be
Such a warm soft sleeping-place
Found for me!

Christina Rossetti

WINTER RAIN

EVERY valley drinks,
  Every dell and hollow;
Where the kind rain sinks and sinks,
  Green of Spring will follow.

Yet a lapse of weeks—
  Buds will burst their edges,
Strip their wool-coats, glue-coats, streaks,
  In the woods and hedges;

Weave a bower of love
  For birds to meet each other,
Weave a canopy above
  Nest and egg and mother.

But for fattening rain
  We should have no flowers,
Never a bud or leaf again
  But for soaking showers;

Never a mated bird
  In the rocking tree-tops,
Never indeed a flock or herd
  To graze upon the lea-crops.

c

Lambs so woolly white,
   Sheep the sun-bright leas on,
They could have no grass to bite
   But for rain in season.

We should find no moss
   In the shadiest places,
Find no waving meadow grass,
   Pied with broad-eyed daisies:

But miles of barren sand,
   With never a son or daughter;
Not a lily on the land,
   Or lily on the water.

Christina Rossetti

HUNTING SONG

(Made for King Henry VIII)

THE hunt is up, the hunt is up,
   And it is well nigh day;
And Harry our King is gone hunting
   To bring his deer to bay.

The east is bright with morning light,
   And darkness it is fled;
And the merry horn wakes up the morn
   To leave his idle bed.

Behold the skies with golden dyes
   Are glowing all around;
The grass is green, and so are the treen
   All laughing at the sound.

The horses snort to be at sport,
    The dogs are running free,
The woods rejoice at the merry noise
    Of *Hey tantara tee ree!*

The sun is glad to see us clad
    All in our lusty green,
And smiles in the sky as he riseth high
    To see and to be seen.

Awake all men, I say again,
    Be merry as you may;
For Harry our King is gone hunting,
    To bring his deer to bay.

Anon.

PEASANTS' HUNTING-SONG

UP, up! ye dames, ye lasses gay!
    To the meadows trip away.
'Tis you must tend the flocks this morn,
And scare the small birds from the corn.
Not a soul at home may stay;
    For the shepherds must go
    With lance and bow
To hunt the wolf in the woods to-day.

Leave the hearth and leave the house
To the cricket and the mouse:
Find grannam out a sunny seat,
With babe and lambkin at her feet.
Not a soul at home may stay:
    For the shepherds must go
    With lance and bow
To hunt the wolf in the woods to-day.

Samuel Taylor Coleridge

THE FAIRIES

U P the airy mountain,
   Down the rushy glen,
We daren't go a-hunting,
   For fear of little men;
Wee folk, good folk,
   Trooping all together;
Green jacket, red cap,
   And white owl's feather!

Down along the rocky shore
   Some make their home,
They live on crispy pancakes
   Of yellow tide-foam;
Some in the reeds
   Of the black mountain-lake,
With frogs for their watch-dogs,
   All night awake.

High on the hill-top
   The old King sits;
He is now so old and gray
   He's nigh lost his wits.
With a bridge of white mist
   Columbkill he crosses,
On his stately journeys
   From Slieveleague to Rosses;
Or going up with music
   On cold starry nights,
To sup with the Queen
   Of the gay Northern Lights.

They stole little Bridget
   For seven years long;
When she came down again
   Her friends were all gone.
They took her lightly back,
   Between the night and morrow,
They thought that she was fast asleep,
   But she was dead with sorrow.
They have kept her ever since,
   Deep within the lakes,
On a bed of flag-leaves,
   Watching till she wakes.

By the craggy hill-side,
   Through the mosses bare
They have planted thorn-trees
   For pleasure here and there.
Is any man so daring
   As dig one up in spite,
He shall find the thornies set
   In his bed at night.

Up the airy mountain,
   Down the rushy glen,
We daren't go a-hunting
   For fear of little men;
Wee folk, good folk,
   Trooping all together;
Green jacket, red cap,
   And white owl's feather!

William Allingham

SONGS OF THE FAIERIES

I

BY the Moon we sport and play,
With the night begins our day:
As we dance the dew doth fall,
Trip it, little urchins all:
Lightly as the little Bee,
Two by two, and three by three:
And about go we, and about go we.

II

Round about, round about, in a fair Ring-a:
Thus we dance, thus we dance, and thus we sing-a:
Trip and go, to and fro, over this Green-a:
All about, in and out, for our brave Queen-a.

We have danc'd round about, in a fair Ring-a:
We have danc'd lustily, and thus we sing-a:
All about, in and out, over this Green-a:
To and fro, trip and go, to our brave Queen-a.

John Lyly?

LULLABY FOR TITANIA

YOU spotted snakes with double tongue,
Thorny hedgehogs, be not seen;
Newts and blind-worms, do no wrong,
Come not near our fairy queen.
Philomel, with melody,
Sing in our sweet lullaby:
Lulla, lulla, lullaby; lulla, lulla, lullaby!
Never harm, nor spell, nor charm,
Come our lovely lady nigh;
So, good-night, with lullaby.

Weaving spiders, come not here:
   Hence, you long-legged spinners, hence!
Beetles black, approach not near;
   Worm, nor snail, do no offence.
      Philomel, with melody,
      Sing in our sweet lullaby:
Lulla, lulla, lullaby; lulla, lulla, lullaby!
      Never harm, nor spell, nor charm,
      Come our lovely lady nigh;
      So, good-night, with lullaby.

from A MIDSUMMER NIGHT'S DREAM   *William Shakespeare*

THE PROUD MYSTERIOUS CAT

(A chant for a pantomime dance)

I SAW a proud, mysterious cat,
  I saw a proud, mysterious cat,
Too proud to catch a mouse or rat—
  Mew, mew, mew.

But catnip, she would eat, and purr,
But catnip, she would eat, and purr,
And goldfish she did much prefer—
  Mew, mew, mew.

I saw a cat—'twas but a dream,
I saw a cat—'twas but a dream,
Who scorned the slave that brought her cream—
  Mew, mew, mew.

Unless the slave were dressed in style,
Unless the slave were dressed in style,
And knelt before her all the while—
  Mew, mew, mew.

27

Did you ever hear of a thing like that?
Did you ever hear of a thing like that?
Did you ever hear of a thing like that?
Oh, what a proud mysterious cat.
Oh, what a proud mysterious cat.
Oh, what a proud mysterious cat.
　　Mew . . . mew . . . mew.

Vachel Lindsay

MIDNIGHT

MIDNIGHT'S bell goes ting, ting, ting, ting, ting,
　　Then dogs do howl, and not a bird does sing
But the nightingale, and she cries twit, twit, twit:
Owls then on every bough do sit;
Ravens croak on chimneys' tops;
The cricket in the chamber hops,
　　And the cats cry mew, mew, mew,
The nibbling mouse is not asleep,
But he goes peep, peep, peep, peep, peep,
　　And the cats cry mew, mew, mew,
　　And still the cats cry mew, mew, mew.

Thomas Middleton

From GOBLIN MARKET

MORNING and evening
　　Maids heard the goblins cry:
"Come buy our orchard fruits,
Come buy, come buy:
Apples and quinces,
Lemons and oranges,
Plump unpecked cherries,
Melons and raspberries,

Bloom-down-cheeked peaches,
Swart-headed mulberries,
Wild free-born cranberries,
Crab-apples, dewberries,
Pine-apples, blackberries,
Apricots, strawberries;—
All ripe together
In summer weather,—
Morns that pass by,
Fair eves that fly
Come buy, come buy:
Our grapes fresh from the vine,
Pomegranates full and fine,
Dates and sharp bullaces,
Rare pears and greengages,
Damsons and bilberries,
Taste them and try:
Currants and gooseberries,
Bright-fire-like barberries,
Figs to fill your mouth,
Citrons from the South,
Sweet to tongue and sound to eye;
Come buy, come buy. . . ."

Christina Rossetti

THE RIDE-BY-NIGHTS

UP on their brooms the Witches stream,
Crooked and black in the crescent's gleam;
One foot high, and one foot low,
Bearded, cloaked, and cowled, they go.
'Neath Charlie's Wane they twitter and tweet,
And away they swarm 'neath the Dragon's feet.
With a whoop and a flutter they swing and sway,
And surge pell-mell down the Milky Way.

Betwixt the legs of the glittering Chair
They hover and squeak in the empty air.
Then round they swoop past the glimmering Lion
To where Sirius barks behind huge Orion;
Up, then, and over to wheel amain,
Under the silver, and home again.

Walter de la Mare

THE TWELVE DAYS OF CHRISTMAS

THE first day of Christmas, my true love sent to me
A partridge in a pear-tree.

The second day of Christmas, my true love sent to me
Two turtle doves and
A partridge in a pear-tree.

The third day of Christmas, my true love sent to me
Three French hens,
Two turtle doves, and
A partridge in a pear-tree.

The fourth day of Christmas, my true love sent to me
Four colly[1] birds,
Three French hens,
Two turtle doves, and
A partridge in a pear-tree.

The fifth day of Christmas, my true love sent to me
Five gold rings,
Four colly birds,
Three French hens,
Two turtle doves, and
A partridge in a pear-tree.

[1] black

The sixth day of Christmas, my true love sent to me
Six geese a-laying,
Five gold rings,
Four colly birds,
Three French hens,
Two turtle doves, and
A partridge in a pear-tree.

The seventh day of Christmas, my true love sent to me
Seven swans a-swimming,
Six, etc.

The eighth day of Christmas, my true love sent to me
Eight maids a-milking,
Seven, etc.

The ninth day of Christmas, my true love sent to me
Nine drummers drumming,
Eight, etc.

The tenth day of Christmas, my true love sent to me
Ten pipers piping,
Nine, etc.

The eleventh day of Christmas, my true love sent to me
Eleven ladies dancing,
Ten, etc.

The twelfth day of Christmas, my true love sent to me
Twelve lords a-leaping,
Eleven ladies dancing,
Ten pipers piping,
Nine drummers drumming,
Eight maids a-milking,
Seven swans a-swimming,

Six geese a-laying,
Five gold rings,
Four colly birds,
Three French hens,
Two turtle doves, and
A partridge in a pear-tree.

Traditional

I SAW THREE SHIPS

I SAW three ships come sailing in
  On Christmas day, on Christmas day;
I saw three ships come sailing in
  On Christmas day in the morning.

And what was in those ships all three,
  On Christmas day, on Christmas day?
And what was in those ships all three,
  On Christmas day in the morning?

Our Saviour Christ and His Lady,
  On Christmas day, on Christmas day;
Our Saviour Christ and His Lady,
  On Christmas day in the morning.

Pray whither sailed those ships all three,
  On Christmas day, on Christmas day?
Pray whither sailed those ships all three,
  On Christmas day in the morning?

O they sailed into Bethlehem,
  On Christmas day, on Christmas day;
O they sailed into Bethlehem,
  On Christmas day in the morning.

And all the bells on earth shall ring,
On Christmas day, on Christmas day;
And all the bells on earth shall ring,
On Christmas day in the morning.

And all the angels in Heaven shall sing,
On Christmas day, on Christmas day;
And all the angels in Heaven shall sing,
On Christmas day in the morning.

And all the souls on earth shall sing,
On Christmas day, on Christmas day;
And all the souls on earth shall sing,
On Christmas day in the morning.

Then let us all rejoice amain,
On Christmas day, on Christmas day;
Then let us all rejoice amain,
On Christmas day in the morning.

Traditional

From *CHRISTMAS: A SONG FOR THE YOUNG AND THE WISE*

CHRISTMAS comes! He comes, he comes,
Ushered with a rain of plums;
Hollies in the windows greet him;
Schools come driving post to meet him;
Gifts precede him, bells proclaim him,
Every mouth delights to name him;
Wet, and cold, and wind, and dark,
Make him but the warmer mark; . . .
Curtains, those snug room-enfolders,
Hang upon his million-shoulders.
And he has a million eyes
Of fire, and eats a million pies,
And is very merry and wise;

Very wise and very merry,
And loves a kiss beneath the berry. . . .
Now is he a green array,
And now an "eve," and now a "day"; . . .
And now the pantomime and clown
With a crack upon the crown,
And all sorts of tumbles down;
And then he's music in the night,
And the money gotten by't: . . .
He's a turkey, he's a goose,
He's oranges unfit for use;
He's a kiss that loves to grow
Underneath the mistletoe;
And he's forfeits, cards, and wassails,
And a king and queen with vassals. . . .
Then, some morning, in the lurch
Leaving romps, he goes to church,
Looking very grave and thankful,
After which he's just as prankful,
Now a saint, and now a sinner,
But, above all, he's a dinner;
He's a dinner, where you see
Everybody's family;
Beef, and pudding, and mince-pies,
And little boys with laughing eyes; . . .
He's a dinner and a fire,
Heaped beyond your heart's desire—
Heaped with log, and baked with coals,
Till it roasts your very souls,
And your cheek the fire outstares,
And you all push back your chairs,
And the mirth becomes too great,
And you all sit up too late,
Nodding all with too much head,
And so go off to too much bed. . . .

Leigh Hunt

WHEN HANNIBAL CROSSED THE ALPS

HANNIBAL crossed the Alps!
  Hannibal crossed the Alps!
 With his black men,
 His brown men,
     His countrymen,
     His town-men,
With his Gauls, and his Spaniards, his horses and elephants,
Hannibal crossed the Alps!

Hannibal crossed the Alps!
Hannibal crossed the Alps!
     For his bowmen,
     His spear-men,
     His front men,
     His rear men,
His Gauls and his Spaniards, his horses and elephants,
Wanted the Roman scalps!
And *that's* why Hannibal, Hannibal, Hannibal,
Hannibal crossed the Alps!

from MIGHTY MEN   *Eleanor Farjeon*

MARCHING SONG

WE be the King's men, hale and hearty,
  Marching to meet one Buonaparty;
If he won't sail, lest the wind should blow,
We shall have marched for nothing, O!
     Right fol-lol!

35

We be the King's men, hale and hearty,
Marching to meet one Buonaparty;
If he be sea-sick, says "No, no!"
We shall have marched for nothing, O!
       Right fol-lol!

We be the King's men, hale and hearty,
Marching to meet one Buonaparty;
Never mind, mates; we'll be merry, though
We may have marched for nothing, O!
       Right fol-lol!

Thomas Hardy

BOLD ROBIN HOOD

OH, bold Robin Hood is a forester good,
   As ever drew bow in the merry greenwood:
At his bugle's shrill singing the echoes are ringing,
The wild deer are springing for many a rood:
Its summons we follow, through brake, over hollow,
The thrice-blown shrill summons of bold Robin Hood.

And what eye hath e'er seen such a sweet Maiden Queen,
As Marion, the pride of the forester's green?
A sweet garden flower, she blooms in the bower,
Where alone to this hour the wild rose has been:
We hail her in duty the queen of all beauty:
We will live, we will die, by our sweet Maiden Queen.

And here's a grey friar, good as heart can desire,
To absolve all our sins as the case may require:
Who with courage so stout, lays his oak-plant about,
And puts to the rout all the foes of his choir:
For we are his choristers, we merry foresters,
Chorusing thus with our militant friar.

And Scarlet doth bring his good yew-bough and string,
Prime minister is he of Robin our king;
No mark is too narrow for Little John's arrow,
That hits a cock-sparrow a mile on the wing:
Robin and Mariòn, Scarlet and Little John,
Long with their glory old Sherwood shall ring.

Each a good liver, for well-feathered quiver
Doth furnish brawn, venison, and fowl of the river:
But the best game we dish up, it is a fat bishop:
When his angels[1] we fish up, he proves a free giver:
For a prelate so lowly has angels more holy,
And should this world's false angels to sinners deliver.

Robin and Mariòn, Scarlet and Little John,
Drink to them one by one, drink as ye sing:
Robin and Mariòn, Scarlet and Little John,
Echo to echo through Sherwood shall fling:
Robin and Mariòn, Scarlet and Little John,
Long with their glory old Sherwood shall ring.

Thomas Love Peacock

LAMENT FOR ROBIN HOOD

WEEP, weep, ye woodmen! wail;
  Your hands with sorrow wring!
Your master Robin Hood lies dead,
  Therefore sigh as you sing.
Here lies his Primer and his beads,
His bent bow and his arrows keen,
His good sword and his holy cross:
Now cast on flowers fresh and green.

[1] *angel*—gold coin worth about 6s 8d

37

D

And, as they fall, shed tears and say
Wella, wella day, wella, wella day!
Thus cast ye flowers fresh and sing,
And on to Wakefield take your way.

Anthony Munday

from THE DEATH OF ROBERT, EARLE OF HUNTINGDON,
OTHERWISE CALLED ROBIN HOOD

COCK UP YOUR BEAVER

WHEN first my brave Johnnie lad
  Came to this town,
He had a blue bonnet
 That wanted the crown;
But now he has gotten
 A hat and a feather,—
Hey, brave Johnnie lad,
 Cock up your beaver!

Cock up your beaver,
 And cock it fu' sprush,
We'll over the Border
 And gi'e them a brush;
There's somebody there
 We'll teach better behaviour,—
Hey, brave Johnnie lad,
 Cock up your beaver!

Robert Burns

A SEA-SONG BY PIRATES

(Made in the reign of Good Queen Bess)

LUSTILY, lustily, let us sail forth,
    The wind trim doth serve us, it blows from the north.
All things we have ready, and nothing we want,
    To furnish our ships that rideth hereby;
Victuals and weapons they be nothing scant,
    Like worthy mariners ourselves we will try.
        Lustily, etc.

The flags be new trimmed, set slanting aloft,
    Our ship for swift swimming, oh she doth excel,
We fear no enemies, we have escaped them oft,
    Of all ships that swimmeth she beareth the bell.
        Lustily, etc.

And here is a master excelleth in skill,
    And our master's mate he is not to seek;
And here is a boatswain will do his good will,
    And here is a ship-boy, we never had leak.
        Lustily, etc.

If fortune then fail not, and our next voyage prove,
    We will return merrily and make good cheer,
And hold all together as friends linked in love,
    The cans shall be filled with wine, ale and beer!
Lustily, lustily, let us sail forth,
The wind trim doth serve us, it blows from the north!

                                                    Anon.

THE FIGHTING TEMERAIRE

IT was eight bells ringing,
   For the morning watch was done,
And the gunner's lads were singing
   As they polished every gun.
It was eight bells ringing,
And the gunner's lads were singing,
For the ship she rode a-swinging
   As they polished every gun.

   Oh! to see the linstock lighting,
      Téméraire! Téméraire!
   Oh! to hear the round shot biting,
      Téméraire! Téméraire!
   Oh! to see the linstock lighting,
   And to hear the round shot biting,
   For we're all in love with fighting
      On the Fighting Téméraire.

It was noontide ringing,
   And the battle just begun,
When the ship her way was winging
   As they loaded every gun.
It was noontide ringing,
When the ship her way was winging,
And the gunner's lads were singing
   As they loaded every gun.

   There'll be many grim and gory,
      Téméraire! Téméraire!
   There'll be few to tell the story,
      Téméraire! Téméraire!
   There'll be many grim and gory,
   There'll be few to tell the story,
   But we'll all be one in glory
      With the Fighting Téméraire!

There's a far bell ringing
  At the setting of the sun,
And a phantom voice is singing
  Of the great days done.
There's a far bell ringing,
And a phantom voice is singing
Of renown for ever clinging
  To the great days done.

   Now the sunset breezes shiver,
      Téméraire! Téméraire!
   And she's fading down the river,
      Téméraire! Téméraire!
   Now the sunset breezes shiver,
   And she's fading down the river,
   But in England's song for ever
      She's the Fighting Téméraire.
                              Sir Henry Newbolt

THE LOBSTER QUADRILLE

"WILL you walk a little faster?" said a whiting to a snail.
"There's a porpoise close behind us, and he's treading on my tail.
See how eagerly the lobsters and the turtles all advance!
They are waiting on the shingle—will you come and join the dance?
   Will you, won't you, will you, won't you, will you join the dance?
   Will you, won't you, will you, won't you, won't you join the dance?

"You can really have no notion how delightful it will be,
When they take us up and throw us, with the lobsters, out
    to sea!"
But the snail replied, "Too far, too far!" and gave a look
    askance—
Said he thanked the whiting kindly, but he would not join
    the dance.
    Would not, could not, would not, could not, would not join
    the dance.
    Would not, could not, would not, could not, could not join
    the dance.

"What matters it how far we go!" his scaly friend replied,
"There is another shore, you know, upon the other side.
The further off from England the nearer is to France—
So turn not pale, beloved snail, but come and join the dance.
    Will you, won't you, will you, won't you, will you join the
    dance?
    Will you, won't you, will you, won't you, won't you join the
    dance?"

from ALICE IN WONDERLAND   *Lewis Carroll*

TURTLE SOUP

"**B**EAUTIFUL Soup, so rich and green,
    Waiting in a hot tureen!
Who for such dainties would not stoop?
Soup of the evening, beautiful Soup!
Soup of the evening, beautiful Soup!
    Beau-ootiful Soo-oop!
    Beau-ootiful Soo-oop!
  Soo-oop of the e-e-evening,
    Beautiful, beautiful Soup!

"Beautiful Soup! Who cares for fish,
Game, or any other dish?

Who would not give all else for two p
ennyworth only of beautiful Soup?
Pennyworth only of beautiful Soup?
    Beau-ootiful Soo-oop!
    Beau-ootiful Soo-oop!
Soo-oop of the e-e-evening,
    Beautiful, beauti-FUL SOUP!"
from ALICE IN WONDERLAND   *Lewis Carroll*

A YEAR'S WINDFALLS

ON the wind of January
   Down flits the snow,
Travelling from the frozen North
   As cold as it can blow.
Poor robin redbreast,
   Look where he comes;
Let him in to feel your fire,
   And toss him of your crumbs.

On the wind in February
   Snowflakes float still,
Half inclined to turn to rain,
   Nipping, dripping, chill.
Then the thaws swell the streams,
   And swollen rivers swell the sea:
If the winter ever ends,
   How pleasant it will be!

In the wind of windy March
   The catkins drop down.
Curly, caterpillar-like,
   Curious green and brown.
With concourse of nest-building birds
   And leaf-buds by the way,
We begin to think of flowers
   And life and nuts some day.

With the gusts of April
　　Rich fruit-tree blossoms fall,
On the hedged-in orchard-green,
　　From the southern wall.
Apple-trees and pear-trees
　　Shed petals white or pink,
Plum-trees and peach-trees;
　　While sharp showers sink and sink.

Little brings the May-breeze
　　Beside pure scent of flowers,
While all things wax and nothing wanes
　　In lengthening daylight hours.
Across the hyacinth beds
　　The wind lags warm and sweet,
Across the hawthorn tops,
　　Across the blades of wheat.

In the wind of sunny June
　　Thrives the red-rose crop,
Every day fresh blossoms blow
　　While the first leaves drop;
White rose and yellow rose
　　And moss rose choice to find,
And the cottage cabbage rose
　　Not one whit behind.

On the blast of scorched July
　　Drives the pelting hail
From thunderous lightning-clouds that blot
　　Blue heaven grown lurid-pale.
Weedy waves are tossed ashore;
　　Sea-things strange to sight
Gasp upon the barren shore
　　And fade away in light.

In the parching August wind
  Corn-fields bow the head,
Sheltered in round valley depths,
  On low hills outspread.
Early leaves drop loitering down
  Weightless on the breeze,
First fruits of the year's decay
  From the withering trees.

In brisk wind of September
  The heavy-headed fruits
Shake upon their bending boughs
  And drop from the shoots;
Some glow golden in the sun,
  Some show green and streaked,
Some set forth a purple bloom,
  Some blush rosy-cheeked.

In strong blast of October,
  At the equinox,
Stirred up in his hollow bed
  Broad ocean rocks;
Plunge the ships on his bosom,
  Leaps and plunges the foam,—
It's oh for mothers' sons at sea,
  That they were safe at home!

In slack wind of November
  The fog forms and shifts;
All the world comes out again
  When the fog lifts.
Loosened from their sapless twigs,
  Leaves drop with every gust;
Drifting, rustling, out of sight
  In the damp or dust.

Last of all, December,
  The year's sands nearly run,
Speeds on the shortest day,
  Curtails the sun;
With its bleak raw wind
  Lays the last leaves low,
Brings back the nightly frosts,
  Brings back the snow.

Christina Rossetti

From *THE SONG OF THE SOWER*

THE maples redden in the sun;
  In autumn gold the beeches stand;
Rest, faithful plough, thy work is done
  Upon the teeming land.
Bordered with trees whose gay leaves fly
On every breath that sweeps the sky,
The fresh dark acres furrowed lie,
  And ask the sower's hand.
Loose the tired steer and let him go
To pasture where the gentians blow,
And we, who till the grateful ground,
Fling we the golden shower around.

Fling wide the generous grain; we fling
O'er the dark mould the green of spring.
For thick the emerald blades shall grow,
When first the March winds melt the snow,
And to the sleeping flowers, below,
  The early bluebirds sing.
Fling wide the grain; we give the fields
  The ears that nod in summer's gale,
The shining stems that summer gilds,
  The harvest that o'erflows the vale,

And swells, an amber sea, between
The full-leaved woods, its shores of green.

Hark! from the murmuring clods I hear
Glad voices of the coming year;
The song of him who binds the grain,
The shout of those that load the wain,
And from the distant grange there comes
    The clatter of the thresher's flail,
And steadily the millstone hums
    Down in the willowy vale.

       *   *   *   *   *

Then, as the garners give thee forth,
    On what glad errands shalt thou go,
Wherever, o'er the waiting earth,
    Roads wind and rivers flow.
The ancient East shall welcome thee
To mighty marts beyond the sea,
And they who dwell where palm groves sound
To summer winds the whole year round,
Shall watch, in gladness, from the shore,
The sails that bring thy glittering store.
                      William Cullen Bryant

WRITTEN IN MARCH

THE Cock is crowing,
    The stream is flowing,
The small birds twitter,
    The lake doth glitter,
The green field sleeps in the sun;
    The oldest and youngest
    Are at work with the strongest;

The cattle are grazing,
Their heads never raising;
There are forty feeding like one!

Like an army defeated
The snow hath retreated,
And now doth fare ill
On the top of the bare hill;
The ploughboy is whooping—anon—anon:
There's joy in the mountains;
There's life in the fountains;
Small clouds are sailing,
Blue sky prevailing;
The rain is over and gone!

William Wordsworth

MAY SONG

ALL in this pleasant evening, together come are we,
For the summer springs so fresh, green and gay;
We tell you of a blossoming and buds on every tree,
Drawing near unto the merry month of May.

Rise up, the master of this house, put on your charm of gold,
For the summer springs so fresh, green and gay;
Be not in pride offended with your name we make so bold,
Drawing near unto the merry month of May.

Rise up, the mistress of this house, with gold along your
breast,
For the summer springs so fresh, green and gay;
And if your body be asleep, we hope your soul's at rest,
Drawing near unto the merry month of May.

48

Rise up, the children of this house, all in your rich attire,
  For the summer springs so fresh, green and gay;
And every hair upon your head shines like the silver wire,
  Drawing near unto the merry month of May.

God bless this house and arbour, your riches and your store,
  For the summer springs so fresh, green and gay;
We hope the Lord will prosper you, both now and ever-
      more,
  Drawing near unto the merry month of May.
                                            Traditional

ADVICE

NOW, you two eyes, that have all night been sleeping,
    Come into the meadows, where the lambs are leaping;
See how they start at every swallow's shadow
That darts across their faces and their meadow.
See how the blades spring upright, when the sun
Takes off the weight of raindrops, one by one.
See how a shower, that freshened leaves of grass,
Can make that bird's voice fresher than it was.
See how the squirrels lash the quiet trees
Into a tempest, where there is no breeze!
Now, you two eyes, that have all night been sleeping,
Come into the meadows, where the lambs are leaping.
                                          W. H. Davies

THE OWL

WHEN cats run home and light is come,
    And dew is cold upon the ground,
And the far-off stream is dumb,

49

And the whirring sail goes round,
And the whirring sail goes round;
  Alone and warming his five wits,
  The white owl in the belfry sits.

When merry milkmaids click the latch,
  And rarely smells the new-mown hay,
And the cock hath sung beneath the thatch
  Twice or thrice his roundelay,
  Twice or thrice his roundelay;
    Alone and warming his five wits,
    The white owl in the belfry sits.

Alfred, Lord Tennyson

LINES AFTER TEA AT GRASMERE

THE sun has long been set,
  The stars are out by twos and threes,
The little birds are piping yet
  Among the bushes and trees;
There's a cuckoo, and one or two thrushes,
And a far-off wind that rushes,
And a sound of water that gushes,
And the cuckoo's sovereign cry
Fills all the hollow of the sky.
  Who would "go parading"
In London, "and masquerading",
On such a night of June
With that beautiful soft half-moon,
And all these innocent blisses?
On such a night as this is!

William Wordsworth

NIGHT OF SPRING

SLOW, horses, slow,
    As thro' the wood we go—
We would count the stars in heaven,
    Hear the grasses grow:

Watch the cloudlets few
Dappling the deep blue,
In our open palms outspread
    Catch the blessèd dew.

Slow, horses, slow,
    As thro' the wood we go—
We would see fair Dian rise
    With her huntress bow:

We would hear the breeze
Ruffling the dim trees,
Hear its sweet love-ditty set
    To endless harmonies.

Slow, horses, slow,
    As thro' the wood we go—
All the beauty of the night
    We would learn and know!

Thomas Westwood

SUMMER

WINTER is cold-hearted,
    Spring is yea and nay.
Autumn is a weathercock
    Blown every way.
Summer days for me
When every leaf is on its tree;

When Robin's not a beggar,
And Jenny Wren's a bride,
And larks hang singing, singing, singing,
Over the wheat-fields wide,
And anchored lilies ride,
And the pendulum spider
Swings from side to side;

And blue-black beetles transact business,
And gnats fly in a host,
And furry caterpillars hasten
That no time be lost,
And moths grow fat and thrive,
And ladybirds arrive.

Before green apples blush,
Before green nuts embrown,
Why one day in the country
Is worth a month in town;
Is worth a day and a year
Of the dusty, musty, lag-last fashion
That days drone elsewhere.

Christina Rossetti

JACK AND JOAN

JACK and Joan they think no ill,
But loving live, and merry still;
Do their week-days' work, and pray
Devoutly on the holy day:
Skip and trip it on the green,
And help to choose the Summer Queen;
Lash out, at a country feast,
Their silver penny with the best.

Well can they judge of nappy ale,
And tell at large a winter tale;
Climb up to the apple loft,
And turn the crabs till they be soft.
Tib is all the father's joy,
And little Tom the mother's boy.
All their pleasure is Content;
And care, to pay their yearly rent.

Joan can call by name her cows,
And deck her window with green boughs;
She can wreaths and tutties[1] make,
And trim with plums a bridal cake.
Jack know what brings gain or loss;
And his long flail can stoutly toss:
Makes the hedge, which others break;
And ever thinks what he doth speak.

Now, you courtly dames and knights,
That study only strange delights;
Though you scorn the homespun gray,
And revel in your rich array;
Though your tongues dissemble deep,
And can your heads from danger keep;
Yet, for all your pomp and train,
Securer lives the silly swain.

Thomas Campion

[1] nosegays

E

BEGGARS' SONG

COME! come away! the Spring
By every bird that can but sing
Or chirp a note, doth now invite
Us forth to taste of his delight,
In field, in grove, on hill, in dale;
But above all the nightingale,
Who in her sweetness strives to outdo
The loudness of the hoarse cuckoo.

Cuckoo! cries he; jug, jug, jug! sings she:
From bush to bush, from tree to tree.
Why in one place then tarry we?

Come away! Why do we stay?
We have no debt or rent to pay;
No bargains or accounts to make;
No land nor lease, to let or take.
Or if we had, should that remove us
When all the world's our own before us,
And where we pass and make resort
It is our kingdom and our court?

Cuckoo! cries he; jug, jug, jug, sings she:
From bush to bush, from tree to tree.
Why in one place then tarry we?

Richard Brome

From *THE SHOEMAKERS' SONG*

HO! workers of the old time styled
The Gentle Craft of Leather!
Young brothers of the ancient guild,
Stand forth once more together!

Call out again your long array,
   In the olden merry manner!
Once more, on gay St Crispin's day,
   Fling out your blazoned banner!

Rap, rap! upon the well-worn stone
   How falls the polished hammer!
Rap, rap! the measured sound has grown
   A quick and merry clamor.
Now shape the sole! now deftly curl
   The glossy vamp around it,
And bless the while the bright-eyed girl
   Whose gentle fingers bound it!

For you, along the Spanish main
   A hundred keels are ploughing;
For you, the Indian on the plain
   His lasso-coil is throwing;
For you, deep glens with hemlock dark
   The woodman's fire is lighting;
For you, upon the oak's gray bark,
   The woodman's axe is smiting.

For you, from Carolina's pine
   The rosin-gum is stealing;
For you, the dark-eyed Florentine
   Her silken skein is reeling;
For you, the dizzy goatherd roams
   His rugged Alpine ledges;
For you, round all her shepherd homes,
   Bloom England's thorny hedges. . . .

Then let the toast be freely quaffed,
   In water cool and brimming,—
"All honor to the good old Craft,
   Its merry men and women!"

Call out again your long array,
    In the old time's pleasant manner;
Once more, on gay St Crispin's day,
    Fling out his blazoned banner!

                    John Greenleaf Whittier

WHERE DO THE GIPSIES COME FROM?

WHERE do the gipsies come from?
    The gipsies come from Egypt.
The fiery sun begot them,
    Their dam was the desert dry.
She lay there stripped and basking,
And gave them suck for the asking,
And an Emperor's bone to play with,
    Whenever she heard them cry.

What did the gipsies do there?
They built a tomb for Pharaoh,
They built a tomb for Pharaoh,
    So tall it touched the sky,
They buried him deep inside it,
Then let what would betide it,
They saddled their lean-ribbed ponies
    And left him there to die.

What do the gipsies do now?
They follow the Sun, their father,
They follow the Sun, their father,
    They know not whither nor why.
Whatever they find they take it,
And if it's a law they break it.
So never you talk to a gipsy,
    Or look in a gipsy's eye.

                    H. H. Bashford

56

WALKING SONG

HERE we go a-walking, so softly, so softly,
  Down the world, round the world, back to London
    town,
To see the waters and the whales, the emus and the man-
    darins,
  To see the Chinese mandarins, each in a silken gown.

Here we go a-walking, so softly, so softly,
  Out by holy Glastonbury, back to London town,
Before a cup, a shining cup, a cup of beating crimson,
  To see Saint Joseph saying mass all with a shaven crown.

And round him are the silly things of hoof and claw and
    feather,
  Upon his right the farm-yard, upon his left the wild;
And all the lambs of all the folds bleat out the Agnus Dei,
  And when he says the holy words he holds the holy Child.

Here we go a-walking, so softly, so softly,
  Through the vast Atlantic waves, back to London town,
To see the ships made whole again that sank below the
    tempest,
  The Trojan and Phœnician ships that long ago went down.

And there are sailors keeping watch on many a Roman galley,
  And silver bars and golden bars and mighty treasure hid,
And splendid Spanish gentlemen majestically walking
  And waiting on their Admiral as once in far Madrid.

Here we go a-walking, so softly, so softly,
  Down and under to New York, back to London town,
To see the face of Liberty that smiles upon all children,
  But when too soon they come of age she answers with a
    frown.

57

And there are all the dancing stars beside the toppling win-
dows,
Human lights and heavenly lights they twinkle side by
side;
There is passing through the streets the mighty voice of
Jefferson
And the armies of George Washington who would not be
denied.

Here we go a-walking, so softly, so softly,
O'er the wide Tibetan plains, back to London town,
To see the youthful Emperor among his seventy princes,
Who bears the mystic sceptre, who wears the mystic
crown.

The tongue he speaks is older far than Hebrew or than
Latin,
And ancient rituals drawn therein his eyes of mercy con,
About his throne the candles shine and thuribles of incense
Are swung about his footstool, and his name is Prester
John.

Here we go a-walking, so softly, so softly,
Down the pass of Himalay, back to London town,
To see our lord most pitiful, the holy Prince Siddartha,
And the Peacock Throne of Akbar, and great Timur
riding down.

Up to Delhi, up to Delhi! lo the Mogul's glory,
Twice ten thousand elephants trumpet round his tent;
Down from Delhi, down from Delhi! lo the leafy budh-tree
Where our lord at the fourth watch received enlighten-
ment.

Here we go a-walking, so softly, so softly,
Through the jungles African, back to London town,

To see the shining rivers and the drinking place by moon-
    light,
And the lions and hyenas and the zebras coming down:

To see bright birds and butterflies, the monstrous hippo-
    potami,
The silent secret crocodiles that keep their ancient guile,
The white road of the caravans that stretches o'er Sahara,
And the Pharaoh in his litter at the fording of the Nile.

Here we go a-walking, so softly, so softly,
Up the holy streets of Rome, back to London town,
To see the marching legions and the Consuls in their
    triumph,
And the moving lips of Virgil, and the laurels of his
    crown.

And there is Cæsar pacing to the foot of Pompey's statue,
All scornful of his mastery, all careless of alarms;
And there the Pope goes all in white, among his scarlet
    Cardinals,
And carried on the shoulders of his gentlemen-at-arms.

Here we go a-walking, so softly, so softly,
Up the hills of Hampstead, back to London town,
And the garden gate stands open and the house door swings
    before us,
And the candles twinkle happily as we lie down.

And here the noble lady is who meets us from our wan-
    derings,
Here are all the sensible and very needful things,
Here are blankets, here is milk, here are rest and slumber,
And the courteous prince of angels with the fire about his
    wings.

Charles Williams

59

SPRING'S WELCOME

WHAT bird so sings, yet so does wail?
   O 'tis the ravish'd nightingale.
Jug, jug, jug, jug, tereu! she cries,
And still her woes at midnight rise.
Brave prick-song! Who is't now we hear?
None but the lark so shrill and clear;
Now at heaven's gate she claps her wings,
The morn not waking till she sings.
Hark, hark, with what a pretty throat
Poor robin redbreast tunes his note!
Hark how the jolly cuckoos sing
Cuckoo! to welcome in the spring!
Cuckoo! to welcome in the spring!

John Lyly

From *CRUSADER CHORUS*

(Men-at-Arms pass, singing)

THE tomb of God before us,
   Our fatherland behind,
Our ships shall leap o'er billows steep,
Before a charmèd wind.

Above our van great angels
Shall fight along the sky;
While martyrs pure and crowned saints
To God for rescue cry.

The red-cross knights and yeomen
Throughout the holy town,
In faith and might, on left and right,
Shall tread the paynim down.

Till on the Mount Moriah
The Pope of Rome shall stand;
The Kaiser and the King of France
Shall guard him on each hand.

There shall he rule all nations,
With crozier and with sword;
And pour on all the heathen
The wrath of Christ the Lord.

(Women-bystanders)

Christ is a rock in the bare salt land,
To shelter our knights from the sun and sand:
Christ the Lord is a summer sun,
To ripen the grain while they are gone. . . .

(Old Knights pass)

Our stormy sun is sinking;
Our sands are running low;
In one fair fight, before the night,
Our hard-worn hearts shall glow.

We cannot pine in cloister;
We cannot fast and pray;
The sword which built our load of guilt
Must wipe that guilt away.

We know the doom before us;
The dangers of the road;
Have mercy, mercy, Jesu blest,
When we lie low in blood. . . .

61

(*Boy-Crusaders pass*)
The Christ-child sits on high:
He looks through the merry blue sky;
He holds in his hand a bright lily-band,
For the boys who for Him die. . . .

(*Young Knights pass*)
The rich East blooms fragrant before us;
All Fairy-land beckons us forth;
We must follow the crane in her flight o'er the main,
From the frosts and the moors of the North.

Our sires in the youth of the nations
Swept westward through plunder and blood,
But a holier quest calls us back to the East,
We fight for the kingdom of God. . . .

(*Old Monk, looking after them*)
Jerusalem, Jerusalem!
The burying place of God!
Why gay and bold, in steel and gold,
O'er the paths where Christ hath trod?

Charles Kingsley

PILGRIM SONG

WHO would true valour see,
Let him come hither;
One here will constant be,
Come Wind, come Weather.
There's no discouragement
Shall make him once relent
His first avow'd intent
To be a Pilgrim.

Who so beset him round
With dismal Stories,
Do but themselves confound,
His Strength the more is;
No Lion can him fright,
He'll with a Giant fight,
But he will have a right
To be a Pilgrim.

Hobgoblin nor foul Fiend
Can daunt his Spirit;
He knows he at the end
Shall Life inherit.
Then Fancies fly away,
He'll fear not what men say,
He'll labour night and day
To be a Pilgrim.

from THE PILGRIM'S PROGRESS   *John Bunyan*

From *SEAWEED*

WHEN descends on the Atlantic
    The gigantic
Storm-wind of the equinox,
Landward in his wrath he scourges
    The toiling surges
Laden with seaweed from the rocks:

From Bermuda's reefs; from edges
    Of sunken ledges,
In some far-off bright Azore;
From Bahama, and the dashing,
    Silver-flashing
Surges of San Salvador;

From the tumbling surf, that buries
   The Orkneyan skerries,
Answering the hoarse Hebrides;
And from wrecks of ships, and drifting
   Spars, uplifting
On the desolate, rainy seas;—

Ever drifting, drifting, drifting
   On the shifting
Currents of the restless main;
Till in sheltered coves, and reaches
   Of sandy beaches,
All have found repose again. . . .

                Henry Wadsworth Longfellow

From *THE SONG OF THE FISHERMEN*

HURRAH! the seaward breezes
   Sweep down the bay amain;
Heave up, my lads, the anchor!
   Run up the sail again!
Leave to the lubber landsmen
   The rail-car and the steed;
The stars of heaven shall guide us,
   The breath of heaven shall speed. . . .

Now, brothers, for the icebergs
   Of frozen Labrador,
Floating spectral in the moonshine,
   Along the low, black shore!
Where like snow the gannet's feathers
   On Brador's rocks are shed,
And the noisy murr are flying,
   Like black scuds, overhead;

Where in mist the rock is hiding,
    And the sharp reef lurks below,
And the white squall smites in summer,
    And the autumn tempests blow;
Where, through gray and rolling vapour,
    From evening unto morn,
A thousand boats are hailing,
    Horn answering unto horn. . . .

Hurrah!—hurrah!—the west-wind
    Comes freshening down the bay,
The rising sails are filling,—
    Give way, my lads, give way!
Leave the coward landsman clinging
    To the dull earth, like a weed,—
The stars of heaven shall guide us,
    The breath of heaven shall speed!

John Greenleaf Whittier

THE GALLEY-ROWERS

STAGGERING over the running combers
    The long-ship heaves her dripping flanks,
Singing together, the sea-roamers
    Drive the oars grunting in the banks.
        A long pull,
        And a long long pull to Mydath.

"Where are ye bound, ye swart sea-farers,
    Vexing the grey wind-angered brine,
Bearers of home-spun cloth, and bearers
    Of goat-skins filled with country wine?"

65

"We are bound sunset-wards, not knowing,
   Over the whale's way miles an miles,
Going to Vine-Land, haply going
   To the Bright Beach of the Blessed Isles.

"In the wind's teeth and the spray's stinging
   Westward and outward forth we go,
Knowing not whither nor why, but singing
   An old old oar-song as we row.
      A long pull,
      And a long long pull to Mydath."

John Masefield

ODE TO THE NORTH-EAST WIND

WELCOME, wild North-easter!
      Shame it is to see
Odes to every zephyr;
      Ne'er a verse to thee.
Welcome, black North-easter!
      O'er the German foam;
O'er the Danish moorlands,
      From thy frozen home.
Tired we are of summer,
      Tired of gaudy glare,
Showers soft and steaming,
      Hot and breathless air.
Tired of listless dreaming,
      Through the lazy day:
Jovial wind of winter
      Turns us out to play!
Sweep the golden reed-beds;
      Crisp the lazy dyke;
Hunger into madness
      Every plunging pike.

Fill the lake with wild-fowl;
    Fill the marsh with snipe;
While on dreary moorlands
    Lonely curlew pipe.
Through the black fir-forest
    Thunder harsh and dry,
Shattering down the snow-flakes
    Off the curdled sky.
Hark! the brave North-easter!
    Breast-high lies the scent,
On by holt and headland,
    Over heath and bent.
Chime, ye dappled darlings,
    Through the sleet and snow.
Who can over-ride you?
    Let the horses go!
Chime, ye dappled darlings,
    Down the roaring blast;
You shall see a fox die
    Ere an hour be past.
Go! and rest to-morrow,
    Hunting in your dreams,
While our skates are ringing
    O'er the frozen streams.
Let the luscious South-wind
    Breathe in lovers' sighs,
While the lazy gallants
    Bask in ladies' eyes.
What does he but soften
    Heart alike and pen?
'Tis the hard grey weather
    Breeds hard English men.
What's the soft South-wester?
    'Tis the ladies' breeze,
Bringing home their true-loves
    Out of all the seas.

But the black North-easter,
    Through the snowstorm hurled,
Drives our English hearts of oak
    Seaward round the world.
Come, as came our fathers,
    Heralded by thee,
Conquering from the eastward,
    Lords by land and sea.
Come; and strong within us
    Stir the Vikings' blood;
Bracing brain and sinew;
    Blow, thou wind of God!

Charles Kingsley

From *SONG OF THE STARS*

AWAY, away, through the wide, wide sky
    The fair blue fields that before us lie,—
Each sun with the worlds that round him roll,
Each planet, poised on her turning pole,
With her isles of green, and her clouds of white,
And her waters that lie like fluid light. . . .

Look, look, through our glittering ranks afar,
In the infinite azure, star after star,
How they brighten and bloom as they swiftly pass!
How the verdure runs o'er each rolling mass!
And the path of the gentle winds is seen,
Where the small waves dance, and the young woods lean.

And see, where the brighter day-beams pour,
How the rainbows hang in the sunny shower;
And the morn and eve, with their pomp of hues,
Shift o'er the bright planets and shed their dews;
And 'twixt them both, o'er the teeming ground,
With her shadowy cone the night goes round! . . .

William Cullen Bryant

THE BROOK

I COME from haunts of coot and hern,
   I make a sudden sally,
And sparkle out among the fern,
   To bicker down a valley.

By thirty hills I hurry down,
   Or slip between the ridges,
By twenty thorps, a little town,
   And half a hundred bridges.

Till last by Philip's farm I flow
   To join the brimming river,
For men may come and men may go,
   But I go on for ever.

I chatter over stony ways,
   In little sharps and trebles,
I bubble into eddying bays,
   I babble on the pebbles.

With many a curve my banks I fret
   By many a field and fallow,
And many a fairy foreland set
   With willow-weed and mallow.

I chatter, chatter, as I flow
   To join the brimming river,
For men may come and men may go,
   But I go on for ever.

I wind about, and in and out,
   With here a blossom sailing,
And here and there a lusty trout,
   And here and there a grayling.

And here and there a foamy flake
   Upon me, as I travel
With many a silvery waterbreak
   Above the golden gravel,

And draw them all along, and flow
   To join the brimming river,
For men may come and men may go,
   But I go on for ever.

I steal by lawns and grassy plots,
   I slide by hazel covers;
I move the sweet forget-me-nots
   That grow for happy lovers.

I slip, I slide, I gloom, I glance,
   Among my skimming swallows;
I make the netted sunbeams dance
   Against my sandy shallows.

I murmur under moon and stars
   In brambly wildernesses;
I linger by my shingly bars;
   I loiter round my cresses;

And out again I curve and flow
   To join the brimming river,
For men may come and men may go,
   But I go on for ever.

               Alfred, Lord Tennyson

SONG OF THE RIVER

CLEAR and cool, clear and cool,
      By laughing shallow, and dreaming pool;
Cool and clear, cool and clear,
By shining shingle, and foaming weir;
Under the crag where the ouzel sings,
And the ivied wall where the church-bell rings,
      Undefiled, for the undefiled;
      Play by me, bathe in me, mother and child.

Dank and foul, dank and foul,
      By the smoky town in its murky cowl;
      Foul and dank, foul and dank,
      By wharf and sewer and slimy bank;
Darker and darker the further I go,
Baser and baser the richer I grow;
      Who dare sport with the sin-defiled?
      Shrink from me, turn from me, mother and child.

      Strong and free, strong and free;
      The flood-gates are open, away to the sea.
      Free and strong, free and strong,
      Cleansing my streams as I hurry along
To the golden sands, and the leaping bar,
And the taintless tide that awaits me afar,
Till I lose myself in the infinite main,
      Like a soul that has sinned and is pardoned again.
      Undefiled, for the undefiled;
      Play by me, bathe in me, mother and child.

from THE WATER-BABIES   *Charles Kingsley*

SONG OF THE CLOUD-NYMPHS

HO! We are the Nepheliads, we,
    Who bring the clouds from the great sea,
And have within our happy care
All the love 'twixt earth and air.
We it is with soft new showers
Wash the eyes of the young flowers;
And with many a silver comer
In the sky delight the summer;
And our bubbling freshness bringing,
Set the thirsty brooks a-singing,
Till they run for joy, and turn
Every mill-wheel down the burn.

We too tread the mightier mass
Of clouds that take whole days to pass;
And are sometimes forced to pick
With fiery arrows through the thick,
Till the cracking racks asunder
Roll, and awe the world with thunder.
Then the seeming freshness shoots,
And clears the air, and cleans the fruits,
And runs, heart-cooling, to the roots.

Sometimes on the shelves of mountains
Do we rest our burly fountains;
Sometimes for a rainbow run
Right before the laughing sun;
And if we slip down to earth
With the rain for change of mirth,
Worn-out winds and pattering leaves
Are what we love; and dripping eaves
Dotting on the sleepy stone;
And a leafy nook and lone,

Where the bark on the small treen
Is with moisture always green;
And lime-tree bowers, and grass-edged lanes
With little ponds that hold the rains,
Where the nice-eyed wagtails glance,
Sipping 'twixt their jerking dance.
But at night in heaven we sleep,
Halting our scattered clouds like sheep;
Or are passed with sovereign eye
By the Moon, who rideth by
With her sidelong face serene,
Like a most benignant queen.

Leigh Hunt

SONG OF THE FAYS

(*On the culprit Fay's return*)

OUPHE and goblin! imp and sprite!
    Elf of eve! and starry Fay!
Ye that love the moon's soft light,
    Hither—hither wend your way;
Twine ye in a jocund ring,
    Sing and trip it merrily,
Hand to hand, and wing to wing,
    Round the wild witch-hazel tree.

Hail the wanderer again,
    With dance and song, and lute and lyre,
Pure his wing and strong his chain,
    And doubly bright his fairy fire—
Twine ye in an airy round,
    Brush the dew, and print the lea;
Skip and gambol, hop and bound,
    Round the wild witch-hazel tree.

The beetle guards our holy ground,
   He flies about the haunted place,
And if mortal there be found,
   He hums in his ears and flaps his face;
The leaf-harp sounds our roundelay,
   The owlet's eyes our lanterns be;
Thus we sing, and dance, and play,
   Round the wild witch-hazel tree.

from THE CULPRIT FAY   *J. R. Drake*

CYCLOPS' SONG

BRAVE iron! brave hammer! from your sound,
   The art of Music has her ground:
On the anvil thou keep'st time,
Thy knick-a-knock is a smith's best chime.
    Yet thwick-a-thwack,
    Thwick, thwack-a-thwack, thwack,
    Make our brawny sinews crack
    Then pit-a-pat, pat, pit-a-pat, pat,
    Till thickest bars be beaten flat.

We shoe the horses of the sun,
Harness the dragons of the moon,
Forge Cupid's quiver, bow and arrows,
And our dame's coach that's drawn with sparrows,
    Till thwick-a-thwack, etc.

Jove's roaring cannons, and his rammers
We beat out with our Lemnian hammers;
Mars his gauntlet, helm and spear,
And Gorgon shield, are all made here.
    Till thwick-a-thwack, etc.

74

The grate which (shut) the day out-bars,
Those golden studs which nail the stars,
The globe's case, and the axle-tree,
Who can hammer these but we—
    Till thwick-a-thwack, etc.

A warming-pan to heat earth's bed,
Lying i' th' frozen zone half dead;
Hob-nails to serve the man i' th' moon,
And sparrowbills to clout Pan's shoon,
    Whose work but ours?
    Till thwick-a-thwack, etc.

Venus' kettles, pots and pans,
We make, or else she brawls and bans;
Tongs, shovels, and irons have their places,
Else she scratches all our faces,
    Till thwick-a-thwack, etc.

Thomas Dekker

THE SEA-FAIRIES

SLOW sail'd the weary mariners and saw,
  Betwixt the green brink and the running foam,
Sweet faces, rounded arms, and bosoms prest
To little harps of gold; and while they mused
Whispering to each other half in fear,
Shrill music reach'd them on the middle sea.

Whither away, whither away, whither away? fly no more.
Whither away from the high green field, and the happy
    blossoming shore?
Day and night to the billow the fountain calls:
Down shower the gambolling waterfalls
From wandering over the lea:

75

Out of the live-green heart of the dells
They freshen the silvery-crimson shells,
And thick with white bells the clover hill swells
High over the full-toned sea:
O hither, come hither and furl your sails,
Come hither to me and to me:
Hither, come hither and frolic and play;
Here it is only the mew that wails;
We will sing to you all the day:
Mariner, mariner, furl your sails,
For here are the blissful downs and dales,
And merrily, merrily carol the gales,
And the spangle dances in bight and bay,
And the rainbow forms and flies on the land
Over the islands free;
And the rainbow lives in the curve of the sand;
Hither, come hither and see;
And the rainbow hangs on the poising wave,
And sweet is the colour of cove and cave,
And sweet shall your welcome be:
O hither, come hither, and be our lords,
For merry brides are we:
We will kiss sweet kisses, and speak sweet words:
O listen, listen, your eyes shall glisten
With pleasure and love and jubilee:
O listen, listen, your eyes shall glisten
When the sharp clear twang of the golden chords
Runs up the ridged sea.
Who can light on as happy a shore
All the world o'er, all the world o'er?
Whither away? listen and stay: mariner, mariner, fly no
    more.

Alfred, Lord Tennyson

Choruses from *THE MASQUE OF PANDORA*

CENTURIES old are the mountains;
  Their foreheads wrinkled and rifted
Helios crowns by day,
Pallid Selene by night;
From their bosoms uptossed
The snows are driven and drifted,
Like Tithonus' beard
Streaming dishevelled and white.

Thunder and tempest of wind
Their trumpets blown in the vastness;
Phantoms of mist and rain,
Cloud and the shadow of cloud,
Pass and repass by the gates
Of their inaccessible fastness;
Ever unmoved they stand,
Solemn, eternal, and proud.

VOICES OF THE WATERS
Flooded by rain and snow
In their inexhaustible sources,
Swollen by affluent streams
Hurrying onward and hurled
Headlong over crags,
The impetuous water-courses
Rush and roar and plunge
Down to the nethermost world.

Say, have the solid rocks
Into streams of silver been melted,
Flowing over the plains,
Spreading to lakes in the fields?

Or have the mountains, the giants,
The ice-helmed, the forest-belted,
Scattered their arms abroad;
Flung in the meadows their shields?

VOICES OF THE WINDS

High on their turreted cliffs
That bolts of thunder have shattered,
Storm-winds muster and blow
Trumpets of terrible breath;
Then from the gateways rush
And before them routed and scattered
Sullen the cloud-rack flies
Pale with the pallor of death.

Onward the hurricane rides,
And flee for shelter the shepherds;
White are the frightened leaves,
Harvests with terror are white:
Panic seizes the herds,
And even the lions and leopards,
Prowling no longer for prey,
Crouch in their caverns with fright.

VOICES OF THE FOREST

Guarding the mountains around
Majestic the forests are standing,
Bright are their crested helms,
Dark is their armour of leaves;
Filled with the breath of freedom
Each bosom subsiding, expanding,
Now like the ocean sinks,
Now like the ocean upheaves.

Planted firm on the rock,
With foreheads stern and defiant,
Loud they shout to the winds,
Loud to the tempest they call;
Naught but Olympian thunders,
That blasted Titan and Giant,
Them can uproot and o'erthrow,
Shaking the earth with their fall.

CHORUS OF OREADES
These are the Voices Three
Of winds and forests and fountains,
Voices of earth and of air,
Murmur and rushing of streams,
Making together one sound,
The mysterious voice of the mountains,
Waking the sluggard that sleeps,
Waking the dreamer of dreams.

These are the Voices Three,
That speak of endless endeavour,
Speak of endurance and strength,
Triumph and fulness of fame,
Sounding about the world,
An inspiration for ever,
Stirring the hearts of men,
Shaping their end and their aim.

Henry Wadsworth Longfellow

TWO CAROLS OF
THE HOLLY AND THE IVY

I

NAY, nay, Ivy!
It may not be, ywis,
For Holly must have the mastery
As the manner is.

Holly beareth berries,
Berries red enow;
The throstlecock, the popinjay
Dance in every bough.

Welaway, sorry Ivy!
What fowls hast thou
But the sorry owlet
That singeth "How, how!"

Ivy beareth berries
As black as any sloe,
There cometh the wood culver,[1]
And feedeth her of tho.[2]

Holly with his merry men
They can dance in hall;
Ivy and her gentle women
Cannot dance at all,

But like a meiny of bullocks
In a waterfall,
Or on a hot summer's day
When they be mad all.

[1] dove   [2] them

Holly and his merry men
  Sit in chairs of gold;
Ivy and her gentle women
  Sit without in fold,

With a pair of kibëd[1]
  Heels caught with cold;
So would I that every man had
  That with Ivy will hold!

  Nay, nay, Ivy!
    It may not be, ywis,
  For Holly must have the mastery
    As the manner is.

II

The holly and the ivy
  Now are both well grown;
Of all the trees that are in the wood
  The holly bears the crown.
    The rising of the sun,
      The running of the deer,
    The playing of the merry organ,
      Sweet singing in the choir.

The holly bears a blossom
  As white as lily flower;
And Mary bore sweet Jesus Christ
  To be our sweet Saviour.
    The rising of the sun,
      The running of the deer,
    The playing of the merry organ,
      Sweet singing in the choir.

[1] with chilblains

The holly bears a berry
  As red as any blood;
And Mary bore sweet Jesus Christ
  To do poor sinners good.
    The rising of the sun, ·
      The running of the deer,
      The playing of the merry organ,
      Sweet singing in the choir.

The holly bears a prickle
  As sharp as any thorn;
And Mary bore sweet Jesus Christ
  On Christmas day in the morn.
    The rising of the sun,
      The running of the deer,
      The playing of the merry organ,
      Sweet singing in the choir.

The holly bears a bark
  As bitter as any gall;
And Mary bore sweet Jesus Christ
  For to redeem us all.
    The rising of the sun,
      The running of the deer,
      The playing of the merry organ,
      Sweet singing in the choir.

The holly and the ivy
  Now are both well grown;
Of all the trees that are in the wood,
  The holly bears the crown.
    The rising of the sun,
      The running of the deer,
      The playing of the merry organ,
      Sweet singing in the choir.

Traditional

I SING OF A MAIDEN

I SING of a maiden
   That is makeless;[1]
King of all kings
   To her Son she ches.[2]
He came all so still
   There His mother was,
As dew in April
   That falleth on the grass.
He came all so still
   To His mother's bower,
As dew in April
   That falleth on the flower.
He came all so still
   Where His mother lay,
As dew in April
   That falleth on the spray.
Mother and maiden
   Was never none but she;
Well may such a lady
   Godës mother be.

Traditional

WHAT CHEER?

WHAT cheer? Good cheer! Good cheer! Good cheer!
   Be merry and glad this good New Year.

Lift up your heartës and be glad!
In Christës birth the angel bade;
Say each to other, if any be sad:
What cheer? Good cheer! Good cheer! Good cheer!
Be merry and glad this good New Year.

      [1] matchless   [2] chose

Now the King of heaven His birth hath take
Joy and mirth we ought to make!
Say each to other, for his sake:
What cheer? Good cheer! Good cheer! Good cheer!
Be merry and glad this good New Year.

I tell you all with heart so free,
Right welcome ye be to me.
Be glad and merry for charity!
What cheer? Good cheer! Good cheer! Good cheer!
Be merry and glad this good New Year.

The goodman of this place in fere[1]
You to be merry he prayeth you here;
And with good heart he doth to you say:
What cheer? Good cheer! Good cheer! Good cheer!
Be merry and glad this good New Year.

Traditional

[1] company

END OF BOOK I

Many Voices

A Collection of Poems
Suitable for Choral Speech

Made by
MONA SWANN

TWO BOOKS IN ONE
BOOK II

PREFACE

THE widespread development of the Choral Speaking of verse has suggested the making of this collection of poems which, in a diversity of ways, voice the thoughts and emotions of the group rather than those of the individual, and are consequently characterized by that impersonality which alone justifies the use of choral speech as a medium of expression.

It must be remembered, however, that choral speech does not necessarily imply unison speech. The multiplicity of ways in which the choir can be adapted to the demands of the poem are as yet hardly explored, but some possibilities are indicated and illustrated in *An Approach to Choral Speech*[1] which has been written as an introduction to the practical use of this anthology.

Many of the poems gathered here are choral in their original intent; some, however—the odes, for example—are choral rather by right of ancestry; for though the *personal* odes of such writers as Shelley and Keats are obviously unsuited to group utterance, this is in no sense alien to the *impersonal* ode, which still retains a spiritual kinship to the choral ode of Greece.

To avoid duplication, the many possible choral poems in the five books of *The Golden Treasury* (Macmillan edition) have been omitted, and are only listed in *An Approach to Choral Speech*; but I have made four exceptions: Nashe's

[1]*An Approach to Choral Speech.* By Mona Swann.

v

'Song of Ver' has not been separated from its neighbouring 'Dirge', and Dryden's 'Song for St Cecilia's Day', Collins's 'Ode to Evening' and Tennyson's 'Choric Song' seemed too precious as examples of their authors' work to be left out for any reason at all. Owing to exigencies of space, also, only some rarer examples of ballads and carols with choral refrains have been included, since in speaking such poems only the soloists actually require copies.

I do not claim that modern poetry is fully represented in this collection. As the art to which it is dedicated is still in an experimental stage, I have felt that, the living poets whose work was included should generally be those who had had some friendly contact with the experiment. I regret that among these Mr Gordon Bottomley is not represented, for his interest in it has been unfailing; but the Choruses in his plays form such an integral part of them that I have not found one that could be severed from its context; this is true, too, of the Choruses in Mr Lascelles Abercrombie's 'Peregrinus' and 'Judith', and, in a somewhat different way, of the 'Stasima' in Mr Wallace Nichols's 'Prometheus in Piccadilly.'

In Mr Bottomley's 'Acts of St Peter', played in Exeter Cathedral last summer and in London this Easter, and in Mr T. S. Eliot's 'The Rock', played at Sadler's Wells this May–June, the spoken chorus has proved its value in the actual stage-production of modern English lyrical drama. If speech-choirs can prove themselves to be increasingly adequate instruments, other poets of to-day may find further use for their potentialities.

MONA SWANN

Moira House
Eastbourne

vi

INDEX OF AUTHORS

BOOK II

INDEX OF TITLES AND FIRST LINES

BOOK II

Titles—*Italics*   First Lines—Roman

INDEX OF TITLES AND FIRST LINES

INDEX OF TITLES AND FIRST LINES

INDEX OF TITLES AND FIRST LINES

INDEX OF TITLES AND FIRST LINES

Three Choruses from the Greek of Euripides
c. 484–407 B.C.

From *THE TROJAN WOMEN*

O MUSE, be near me now, and make
    A strange song for Ilion's sake,
Till a tone of tears be about mine ears,
And out of my lips a music break
For Troy, Troy, and the end of the years:
  When the wheels of the Greek above me pressed,
  And the mighty horse-hoofs beat my breast;
And all around were the Argive spears;
A towering steed of golden rein—
  O gold without, dark steel within—
Ramped at our gates; and all the plain
  Lay silent where the Greeks had been.
And a cry broke from all the folk
Gathered above on Ilion's rock:
  'Up, up, O fear is over now!
  To Pallas, who hath saved us living,
To Pallas bear this victory-vow!'
Then rose the old man from his room,
The merry damsel left her room,
And each bound death about his brow
  With minstrelsy and high thanksgiving!

O, swift were all in Troy that day,
And girt them to the portal-way,
Marvelling at that mountain Thing
Smooth-carven, where the Argives lay,
And wrath, and Ilion's vanquishing:

Meet gift for her that spareth not,
Heaven's yokeless Rider. Up they brought
Through the steep gates her offering:
Like some dark ship that climbs the shore
    On straining cables, up, where stood
Her marble throne, her hallowed floor,
    Who lusted for her people's blood.

A very weariness of joy
Fell with the evening over Troy:
And lutes of Afric mingled there
    With Phrygian songs: and many a maiden,
With white feet glancing light as air,
Made happy music through the gloom:
And fires on many an inward room
All night broad-flashing, flung their glare
    On laughing eyes and slumber-laden.

A Maiden

I was among the dancers there
    To Artemis, and glorying sang
Her of the Hills, the Maid most fair,
    Daughter of Zeus: and lo, there rang
A shout out of the dark, and fell
    Deathlike from street to street, and made
A silence in the citadel:
    And a child cried, as if afraid,
And hid him in his mother's veil.
    Then stalked the Slayer from his den,
The hand of Pallas served her well!
    O blood, blood of Troy was deep
    About the streets and altars then:
And in the wedded rooms of sleep,
    Lo, the desolate dark alone,
    And headless things men stumbled on.

18

And forth, lo, the women go,
The crown of War, the crown of Woe,
To bear the children of the foe
And weep, weep, for Ilion.

translated by Gilbert Murray

From *THE IPHIGENIA IN TAURIS*

CHORUS OF CAPTIVE GREEK WOMEN
on hearing of Iphigenia's planned escape to Greece

Strophe 1

BIRD of the sea-rocks, of the bursting spray,
   O halcyon bird,
That wheelest crying, crying, on thy way;
Who knoweth grief can read the tale of thee:
   One love long lost, one song for ever heard
      And wings that sweep the sea.

Sister, I too beside the sea complain,
   A bird that hath no wing.
Oh, for a kind Greek market-place again,
For Artemis that healeth woman's pain;
   Here I stand hungering.
Give me the little hill above the sea,
The palm of Delos fringèd delicately,
The young sweet laurel and the olive-tree
   Grey-leaved and glimmering;
O Isle of Leto, Isle of pain and love;
The Orbèd Water and the spell thereof;
Where still the Swan, minstrel of things to be,
   Doth serve the Muse and sing!

Ah, the old tears, the old and blinding tears
    I gave God then,
When my town fell, and noise was in mine ears
Of crashing towers, and forth they guided me
Through spears and lifted oars and angry men
    Out to an unknown sea.
They bought my flesh with gold, and sore afraid
    I came to this dark East
To serve, in thrall to Agamemnon's maid,
This Huntress Artemis, to whom is paid
    The blood of no slain beast;
Yet all is bloody where I dwell, Ah me!
Envying, envying that misery
That through all life hath endured changelessly.
    For hard things borne from birth
Make iron of man's heart, and hurt the less.
'Tis change that paineth; and the bitterness
Of life's decay when joy hath ceased to be
    That makes dark all the earth.

Strophe 2

    Behold,
    Two score and ten there be
    Rowers that row for thee,
And a wild hill air, as if Pan were there,
    Shall sound on the Argive sea,
    Piping to set thee free.

    Or is it the stricken string
    Of Apollo's lyre doth sing
Joyously, as he guideth thee
    To Athens, the land of spring;
    While I wait wearying?

Oh, the wind and the oar,
When the great sail swells before,
With sheets astrain, like a horse on the rein,
And on, through the race and roar,
She feels for the farther shore.

Antistrophe 2

Ah me,
To rise upon wings and hold
Straight on up the steeps of gold
Where the joyous Sun in fire doth run,
Till the wings should faint and fold
O'er the house that was mine of old:

Or watch where the glade below
With a marriage dance doth glow,
And a child will glide from her mother's side
Out, out, where the dancers flow:
As I did, long ago.

Oh, battles of gold, and rare
Raiment and starrèd hair,
And bright veils crossed amid tresses tossed
In a dusk of dancing air!
O Youth and the days that were!

translated by Gilbert Murray

From *THE BACCHAE*

Some Maidens

WILL they ever come to me, ever again,
The long long dances,
On through the dark till the dim stars wane?
Shall I feel the dew on my throat, and the stream
Of wind in my hair? Shall our white feet gleam
In the dim expanses?

Oh, feet of a fawn to the greenwood fled,
    Alone in the grass and the loveliness;
Leap of the hunted, no more in dread,
    Beyond the snares and the deadly press:
Yet a voice still in the distance sounds,
A voice and a fear and a haste of hounds;
O wildly labouring, fiercely fleet,
    Onward yet by river and glen, . . .
Is it joy or terror, ye storm-swift feet?
    To the dear lone lands untroubled of men,
Where no voice sounds, and amid the shadowy green
The little things of the woodland live unseen.

What else is Wisdom? What of man's endeavour
    Or God's high grace, so lovely and so great?
    To stand from fear set free, to breathe and wait;
    To hold a hand uplifted over Hate;
And shall not Loveliness be loved for ever?

Others

O Strength of God, slow art thou and still,
    Yet failest never!
On them that worship the Ruthless Will,
On them that dream, doth His judgment wait.
Dreams of the proud man, making great
    And greater ever,
Things which are not of God. In wide
    And devious coverts, hunter-wise,
He coucheth Time's unhasting stride,
    Following, following, him whose eyes
Look not to Heaven. For all is vain,
The pulse of the heart, the plot of the brain,
That striveth beyond the laws that live.
And is thy Faith so much to give,
Is it so hard a thing to see,
    That the Spirit of God, whate'er it be,

The Law that abides and changes not, ages long,
The Eternal and Nature-born—these things be strong?

What else is Wisdom? What of man's endeavour
    Or God's high grace, so lovely and so great?
    To stand from fear set free, to breathe and wait;
    To hold a hand uplifted over Hate;
And shall not Loveliness be loved for ever?

translated by Gilbert Murray

From the Gaelic
HEBRIDEAN SEA-PRAYER

Helmsman	BLEST be the boat.
Crew	God the Father bless her.
Helmsman	Blest be the boat.
Crew	God the Son bless her.
Helmsman	Blest be the boat
Crew	God the Spirit bless her.
All	God the Father, God the Son, God the Spirit Bless the boat.
Helmsman	What can befall you And God the Father with you?
Crew	No harm can befall us.
Helmsman	What can befall you And God the Son with you?
Crew	No harm can befall us.
Helmsman	What can befall you And God the Spirit with you?

Crew	No harm can befall us.
All	God the Father, God the Son, God the Spirit With us eternally.
Helmsman	What can cause you anxiety And the God of the elements over you?
Crew	No anxiety can be ours.
Helmsman	What can cause you anxiety And the King of the elements over you?
Crew	No anxiety can be ours.
Helmsman	What can cause you anxiety And the Spirit of the elements over you?
Crew	No anxiety can be ours.
All	The God of the elements, The King of the elements, The Spirit of the elements Close over us, ever eternally. *Traditional* *translated by Alexander Carmichael*

From the Anglo-Saxon
THE STORM ON SEA

WHILES, my way I take, how men ween it not,
  Under seething of the surges, seeking out the earth,
Ocean's deep abyss; all a-stirred the sea is.
Urged the flood is then, whirled the foam on high,
Fiercely wails the whale-mere, wrathful roars aloud;
Beat the sea-streams on the shore, shooting momently on
     high,
Upon the soaring cliffs, with the sand and stone,
With the weed and wave. But I, warring on,
Shrouded with the ocean's mass, stir into the earth
Into vasty sea-grounds! From the water's helm

24

I may not on journey loose me, ere he let me go
Who my master is.—Say, O man of thought,
Who may draw me (like a sword) from the bosomed depths
    of ocean,
When the streams again on the sea are still,
And the waters silent that shrouded me before?

translated by Stopford A. Brooke

From the Italian of Saint Francis of Assisi
1182–1226

THE CANTICLE OF BROTHER SUN

MOST High Omnipotent Good Lord,
    Thine be the praise and the glory and the honour
    and every benediction.
To thee alone, most High, do they belong,
And there is no man worthy to mention them to thee.

Praised be thou, my Lord, with all thy creatures,
    Especially our brother master Sun,
    Which illumineth for us the day;
    And he is beautiful and radiant with great Splendour;
    Of thee, most High, he beareth the significance.
Praised be thou, my Lord, for our sister Moon and the
      Stars;
    In the sky thou hast made them clear and precious and
      beautiful.
Praised be thou, my Lord, for brother Wind,
    And for cloudy and clear skies and for every weather
    By which to thy creatures thou givest sustenance.
Praised be thou, my Lord, for sister Water,
    Which is very useful and humble and precious and chaste.
Praised be thou, my Lord, for brother Fire,
    By which thou illuminest for us the night,
    And he is beautiful and jocund and robust and strong.

25

Praised be thou, my Lord, for our sister Mother Earth,
　　Which sustaineth us and governeth us,
　　　And bringeth forth divers fruits and coloured flowers and
　　　　leaves.
Praised be thou, my Lord, for those that give pardon by thy
　　love,
　　　And sustain infirmity and tribulation:
　　　Blessed be those that sustain them in peace,
　　　For by thee, most High, they shall be crowned.
Praised be thou, my Lord, for our sister the Death of the
　　body,
　　　From which no man living can escape;
　　　Woe to them that die in mortal sin;
　　　Blessed be those that shall be found in thy most holy will,
　　　For the second death shall do to them no ill.

Let us praise and bless my Lord and give him thanks,
　　And serve him with great humility.　Amen.

translated by Mona Swann

John Wycliffe
1324?–1384
From *ISAIAH LII*

RISE, rise, be clad, thou Sion, with thy strengthe;
　　Be thou clad with the clothis of thy glorie,
Thou Jerusalem, citee of the holi;
For a man uncircumcided and a man uncleene schal no
　　more lie to,
That he pass by thee.
Jerusalem, be thou schaken out of the dust;
Rise thou, sitte thou;
Thou daughter of Sion, prisoner,
Unbynde the bondis of thy necke . . .
. . . Ful faire ben the feet of him that tellith, and prechith
　　peace on hillis,
Of him that tellith good,
　　26

Of him that prechith helthe, and seithe,
Sion, thy God schal regne . . .
. . . Joyeth, and preiseth togidere, ye desertes of Jerusalem;
For the Lord hath comfortid his people,
He hath again bought Jerusalem.
The Lord hath made his holi arm in the eyen of alle folkis,
And alle the endis of the erthe schulen see the helthe of our
    God. . . .
. . . For ye schulen not go out in noyse,
Nether ye schulen haste in fleynge away;
For why the Lord schal go bifore you,
And the God of Israel schal gadere you togidere.
. . . Lo! my servaunt schal undirstonde,
And he schal be enhaunsid,
And he schal be reisid,
And he schal be full high.
He schal besprenge[1] many folkis;
Kingis schulen hold togidere her[2] mouth on him;
For to whom is not told of him, schul see,
And they that herden not, bihelden.

Geoffrey Chaucer
1340?-1400
ROUNDEL
(Sung by the Birds to do Nature honour)

Qui bien aime a tard oublie

NOW welcom somer, with thy sonnë softe,
    That hast this wintres weders over-shake,
And driven awey the longë nightës blake!

Seynt Valentyn, that art ful hy onlofte;—
Thus singen smalë foulës for thy sake—
    Now welcom somer, with thy sonnë softe,
    That hast this wintres weders over-shake.

[1] sprinkle   [2] their

27

Wel han they cause for to gladen ofte,
Sith ech of hem recovered hath his make;
Ful blisful may they singen whan they wake;
Now welcom somer, with thy sonnë softe,
That hast this wintres weders over-shake,
And driven awey the longe nightes blake.

from THE PARLEMENT OF FOULES

Songs and Carols
15th and early 16th cent.

THE SONG OF AGINCOURT

Deo gracias Anglia
Redde pro victoria.

OUR king went forth to Normandy
with grace and might of chivalry:
there God for him wrought marvellously
wherefore Englonde may call and cry,
Deo gracias.

He set a siege the sooth for to say,
to Harflu town with royal array:
that town we won and made affray,
that France shall rue till domësday.
Deo gracias.

Than[1] went our king with all his host,
through France for all the Frenshë boast:
he spared no drede of least or most,
till he came to Agincourt coast.
Deo gracias.

[1] then

28

Than forsooth that knight comely,
In Agincourt he fought manly:
through grace of God most mighty, he
had both the field and the victory.
>   *Deo gracias.*

There dukes and earls, lord and baron,
were take and slain, and that well soon:
and some were led into London,
with joy and mirth and great renown,
>   *Deo gracias.*

Now gracious God he save our king,
his people and all his well-willing:
give him good life and good ending,
that we with mirth may safely sing
>   *Deo gracias.*

>   *Deo gracias Anglia*
>   *Redde pro victoria.*

>> *Anon.*

A 'HUNT UP'

T HE hunt is up, the hunt is up,
>   *Sing merrily we, the hunt is up.*

The birds they sing,
The deer they fling,
>   Hey, nony, nony-no:
The hounds they cry,
The hunters they fly,
>   Hey, trolilo, trololilo.
The hunt is up, the hunt is up,
Sing merrily we, the hunt is up.

The wood resounds,
To hear the hounds,
   Hey, nony, nony-no;
The rocks report
This merry sport,
   Hey, trolilo, trololilo.
The hunt is up, the hunt is up,
Sing merrily we, the hunt is up.

Then hye apace
Unto the chase,
   Hey, nony, nony-no:
Whilst everything
Doth sweetly sing
   Hey, trolilo, trololilo.
The hunt is up, the hunt is up,
Sing merrily we, the hunt is up.

Anon.

THE MAID OF THE MOOR

MAIDEN in the moor lay,
  In the moor lay,
Sennight full and a day.
What was her meat?
What was her meat?
  The primrose and the violet,
  The primrose and the violet.
What was her drink?
  The cold water of the well-spring,
What was her bower?
  The red rose and the lily flower.

from BODLEIAN MS.   *Traditional*

O LUSTY MAY

O LUSTY May, with Flora queen!
The balmy drops from Phœbus sheen
Preluciand beams before the day:
By that Diana growis green
Through gladness of this lusty May.

Then Esperus, that is so bright,
Till[1] woful heartës casts his light,
With banks that blooms on every brae,
And showers are shed forth of their sight,
Through gladness of this lusty May.

Birds on bewis[2] of every birth,
Rejoicing notes makand their mirth
Right pleasantly upon the spray,
With flourishings o'er field and firth,
Through gladness of this lusty May.

All luvaris that are in care
To their ladies they do repair,
In fresh mornings before the day,
And are in mirth aye mair and mair
Through gladness of this lusty May.

from THE BANNATYNE MS.   *Anon.*

          [1] into   [2] boughs

BRING US IN GOOD ALE

BRING us in good ale, and bring us in good ale;
For our blessed Lady sake bring us in good ale!

BRING us in no brown bread, for that is made of bran,
Nor bring us in no white bread, for therein is no gain,
But bring us in good ale!

Bring us in no beef, for there is many bones,
But bring us in good ale, for that goth down at once,
And bring us in good ale!

Bring us in no bacon, for that is passing fat,
But bring us in good ale, and give us enought of that;
And bring us in good ale!

Bring us in no mutton, for that is often lean,
Nor bring us in no tripes, for they be seldom clean,
But bring us in good ale!

Bring us in no egges, for there are many shells,
But bring us in good ale, and give us nothing else;
And bring us in good ale!

Bring us in no butter, for therein are many hairs,
Nor bring us in no pigges flesh, for that will make us bores,
But bring us in good ale!

Bring us in no puddings, for therein is all God's good,[1]
Nor bring us in no venison, for that is not for our blood;
But bring us in good ale!

Bring us in no capons' flesh, for that is ofté dear,
Nor bring us in no duckes flesh, for they slobber in the mere,
But bring us in good ale!

Traditional

[1] yeast

BEAR A HORN AND BLOW IT NAUGHT

I hold him wise and well itaught,
Can bear an horn and blow it naught.

BLOWING was made for gretë game;
Of thy blowing cometh mickle grame;[1]
Therefore I hold it for no shame
To bear a horn and blow it naught.

Hornës are made both loud and shill;[2]
Whan time is, blow thou thy fill,
And whan need is, hold thee still,
And bear a horn and blow it naught.

What so ever be in thy thought,
Here and see and say right nought;
Then shall men say thou art well taught
To bear a horn and blow it naught.

Of all the riches under the sun,
Then was there never better one
Than is a taught man for to con[3]
To bear a horn and blow it naught.

What so ever be in thy breast,
Stop thy mouth with thy fist,
And look thou think well of had-I-wist,
And bear a horn and blow it naught.

And whan thou sittest at the ale,
And criest like a nightingale,
Be ware to whom thou tellest thy tale,
But bear a horn and blow it naught.

Traditional

[1] evil   [2] shrill   [3] know how

C   33

KEEP THY TONGUE

Keepë thy tongue, thy tongue, thy tongue,
Thy wicked tongue worketh me woe.

THERE is none grass that groweth on ground,
    Satenas nor penny round,[1]
Worse than is a wicked tongue,
    That speaketh both evil of friend and foe.

Wicked tongue maketh oftë strife
Betwixt a good man and his wife;
When he should lead a merry life
    Her white sidës waxen full blo.[2]

Wicked tongue maketh oftë staunce[3]
Both in Engelond and in Fraunce.
Many a man with spear and launce,
    Through wicked tongue, to dead is do.[4]

Wicked tonguë breaketh bone,
Though the tonguës self have none,
Of his friend he maketh his fone[5]
    In every place where that he go.

Good men that standen and sitten in this hall,
I pray you both one and all,
That wicked tonguës from you fall,
    That ye moun to heavenë go.

Keepë thy tongue, thy tongue, thy tongue,
Thy wicked tongue worketh me woe.

                Traditional

[1] *Satenas, penny (round?)* = weedy growths.
[2] black and blue
[3] stoppage   [4] done   [5] foes

ADAM LAY YBOUNDEN

ADAM lay ybounden,
  Bounden in a bond;
Four thousand winter
  Thought he not too long;
And all was for an apple,
  An apple that he took,
As clerkës finden
  Written in their book.
Ne had the apple taken been,
  The apple taken been,
Ne haddë never our lady
  A-been hevenë queen.
Blessëd be the time
  That apple taken was.
Therefore we moun[1] sing
  'Deo gracias.'

Traditional

TYRLE, TYRLOW

Tyrle, tyrlow, tyrle, tyrlow,
So merrily the shepherds began to blow!

ABOUT the field they pipëd right,
  So merrily the shepherds began to blow;
Adown from heaven they saw come a light.
  Tyrle, tyrlow, tyrle, tyrlow.

[1] may

Of angels there came a company
With merry songs and melody;
The shepherds anon gan them aspy.
Tyrle, tyrlow, tyrle, tyrlow.

"*Gloria in excelsis*" the angels sang
And said that peace was present among
To every man that to the faith would long.
Tyrle, tyrlow, tyrle, tyrlow.

The shepherds hied them to Bethleme,
To see that blessëd sonnës beam;
And there they found that glorious stream.[1]
Tyrle, tyrlow, tyrle, tyrlow.

Now pray we to that meekë child,
And to his mother that is so mild,
The which was never defiled,
Tyrle, tyrlow, tyrle, tyrlow.

That we may come unto his bliss,
Where joy shall never miss,
Then may we sing in Paradise,
Tyrle, tyrlow, tyrle, tyrlow.

I pray you all that be here,
For to sing and make good cheer,
In the worship of God this year:
Tyrle, tyrlow, tyrle, tyrlow.

Traditional

[1] ray of light

LULLAY, MINE LIKING

Lullay, mine liking, my dear son, mine sweting,
Lullay, my dear heart, mine own dear darling!

I SAW a fair maiden
  Sitten and sing,
She lullëd a little child,
  A sweetë lording.
    Lullay, etc.

That echë[1] lord is that
  That made allë thing;
Of allë lordës he is lord,
  Of allë kingës king.
    Lullay, etc.

There was mickle melody
  At that childës birth;
Allë that were in heaven's bliss
  They made mickle mirth.
    Lullay, etc.

Angels bright they sang that night,
  And saiden to that child,
"Blessëd be thou, and so be she
  That is both meek and mild."
    Lullay, etc.

Pray we now to that child,
  And to his mother dear,
Grant them his blessing
  That now maken cheer.
    Lullay, etc.

Traditional

[1] eternal

A LADY THAT WAS SO FAIR

A LADY that was so fair and bright,
    Velut maris stella,
Brought forth Jesu full of might,
    Parens et puella.

Lady, flower of allë thing,
    Rosa sine spina,
That barest Jesu, Heaven-King,
    Gracia Divina.

All this worldë was forlore,
    Eva peccatrice,
Till that Jesu was ybore,
    De te, genetrice.

Of all women thou art best,
    Felix fecundata,
To all weary thou art rest,
    Mater honorata.

Well I wot He is thy Son,
    Ventre quem portasti;
There will He grant thee thy boon,
    Infans quem lactasti.

How sweet He is, how meek He is
    Nullus memoravit;
In heaven He is and heaven[ly] bliss
    Nobis preparavit.

Of all women thou bearest the prize,
    Mater gratiosa,
Grant us allë Paradise,
    Virgo gloriosa.

Traditional

38

WELCOME YULE

Welcome Yule, thou merry man,
In worship of this holy day!

WELCOME be thou, heavenë king,
    Welcome, born in one morwening,
Welcome, for whom we shall sing,
    Welcome, Yule!

Welcome be ye, Steven and John,
Welcome, Innocents everyone,
Welcome, Thomas, martyr one,
    Welcome, Yule!

Welcome be ye, good New Year,
Welcome, Twelfth Day, both in fere,[1]
Welcome, saintës lefe[2] and dear,
    Welcome, Yule!

Welcome be ye, Candlemasse,
Welcome be ye, Queen of bliss,
Welcome both to more and less,
    Welcome, Yule!

Welcome be ye that arn here,
Welcome all and make good cheer,
Welcome all another year,
    Welcome, Yule!

Welcome, Yule, thou merry man,
In worship of this holy day!

Traditional

    [1] together   [2] dear

"QUID PETIS, O FILI?"

"Quid petis, O Fili?"
Mater dulcissima ba ba:
"Quid petis, O Fili?
Michi plausus oscula da da!"

SO laughing in lap laid,
   So prettily, so pertly,
So passingly well apaid,[1]
Full softly and full soberly,
Unto her sweet Son she said:
   "Quid petis, O Fili?" etc.

The mother full mannerly and meekly as a maid,
Looking on her little Son so laughing in lap laid,
So prettily, so pertly, so passingly well apaid,
So passingly well apaid,
Full softly and full soberly,
Unto her Son she said:
   "Quid petis, O Fili?" etc.

I mean this by Mary, our Maker's mother of light,
Full lovely looking on our Lord, the Lantern of light,
Thus saying to our Saviour, this saw I in my sight;
This reason that I rede in now, I rede it full right.
   "Quid petis, O Fili?" etc.

Musing on her manners so, my word was my main,
Save it pleased me so passingly that past was my pain;
Yet softly to her sweet Son methought I heard her sayn:
"Now gracious God, and good sweet Babe, yet once again
         this game,

---

[1] pleased

40

"*Quid petis, O Fili?*"
Mater dulcissima ba ba :
"*Quid petis, O Fili?*
Michi plausus oscula da da!"

Anon. (*temp*. Henry VII or VIII)

WASSAIL

WASSAIL, wassail, out of the milk pail,
Wassail, wassail, as white as my nail,
Wassail, wassail, in snow, frost and hail,
Wassail, wassail, with partriche and rail,
Wassail, wassail, that much doth avail,
Wassail, wassail, that never will fail.

from KYNGE JOHAN   *John Bale* (1495–1563)

PLEASURE IT IS

PLEASURE it is
   To hear, iwis,
    The birdës sing.
The deer in the dale,
The sheep in the vale,
   The corn springing;
God's purveyance
For sustenance
   It is for man.
Then we always
To him give praise,
   And thank him than,
   And thank him than.

William Cornish (*c*. 1510)

Songs from the Elizabethan Dramas and Song-Books

BEE-SONG

BUZZ, buzz, buzz!
Ring out your kettle
Of purest metal
To settle, to settle,
Your swarm of bees!
For men new wiving
The way to be thriving
Is hiving, hiving;
Then no time leese
To hive your bees.

Anon.

COMING HOMEWARD OUT OF SPAIN

O RAGING Seas,
and mighty Neptune's fane,
In monstrous hills
that knowest thyself so high,
that with thy floods
Dost beat the shores of Spain:
And break the Cliffs
that dare thy force annoy.

Cease now thy rage,
and lay thine ire aside,
And Thou that hast
the governance of all,
O mighty God,
Grant weather, wind and tide,
till on my Country Coast
our anchor fall.

Barnaby Googe (pub. 1563)

MAY

WHEN May is in his prime, then may each heart re-
       joice:
When May bedecks each branch with green, each bird
    strains forth his voice.
The lively sap creeps up into the blooming thorn:
The flowers, which cold in prison kept, now laugh the frost
    to scorn.
All Nature's imps[1] triumph whiles joyful May doth last;
When May is gone, of all the year the pleasant time is past.

May makes the cheerful hue, May breeds and brings new
    blood,
May marcheth throughout every limb, May makes the
    merry mood.
May pricketh tender hearts their warbling notes to tune.
Full strange it is, yet some, we see, do make their May in
    June.
Thus things are strangely wrought, whiles joyful May doth
    last.
Take May in time: when May is gone, the pleasant time is
    past.

All ye that live on earth, and have your May at will,
Rejoice in May, as I do now, and use your May with skill.
Use May while that you may, for May hath but his time;
When all the fruit is gone, it is too late the tree to climb.
Your liking and your lust is fresh while May doth last:
When May is gone, of all the year the pleasant time is past.

from A PARADISE OF DAINTIE DEVICES (1576) *Richard Edwardes*

[1] sons

43

A PROPER SONNET, HOW TIME CONSUMETH
ALL EARTHLY THINGS

AY me, ay me, I sigh to see the scythe afield.
   Down goeth the grass, soon wrought to withered hay;
Ay me, alas, ay me, alas, that beauty needs must yield
   And princes pass, as grass doth fade away.

Ay me, ay me, that life cannot have lasting leave,
   Nor gold take hold of everlasting joy:
Ay me, alas, ay me, alas, that Time hath talents to receive,
   And yet no Time can make a suer[1] stay.

Ay me, ay me, that wit cannot have wishëd choice,
   Nor wish can win, that will desires to see:
Ay me, alas, ay me, alas, that mirth can promise no rejoice,
   Nor study tell what afterward shall be.

Ay me, ay me, that no sure staff is given to age
   Nor age can give sure wit that youth can take:
Ay me, alas, ay me, alas, that no counsel wise and sage
   Will shun the show, that all doth mar and make.

Ay me, ay me, come Time, shear on, and shake the hay,
   It is no boot to baulke thy bitter blows:
Ay me, alas, aye me, alas, come Time, take everything away,
   For all is Thine, be it good or bad, that grows.

from A GORGEOUS GALLERY OF GALLANT INVENTIONS (1578)

[1] *suer* =sure (disyllabic)

44

THE SHOE-MAKERS' SONG

WOULD God that it were holiday!
  Hey derry down, down derry,
That with my Love I might go play;
  With woe my heart is weary;
My whole delight is in her sight,
  Would God I had her company,
          Her company,
Hey derry down, down adown.

My Love is fine, my Love is fair,
  Hey derry down, down derry,
No maid with her may well compare,
  In Kent or Canterbury;
From me my Love shall never move,
  Would God I had her company,
          Her company,
Hey derry down, down adown.

To see her laugh, to see her smile,
  Hey derry down, down derry,
Doth all my sorrows clean beguile,
  And makes my heart full merry;
No grief doth grow where she doth go,
  Would God I had her company,
          Her company,
Hey derry down, down adown.

When I do meet her on the green,
  Hey derry down, down derry,
Methinks she looks like beauty's queen,
  Which makes my heart full merry;

Then I her greet with kisses sweet;
  Would God I had her company,
                Her company,
  Hey derry down, down adown.

My Love comes not of churlish kind,
  Hey derry down, down derry,
But bears a gentle courteous mind,
  Which makes my heart full merry;
She is not coy, she is my joy,
  Would God I had her company,
                Her company,
  Hey derry down, down adown.

Till Sunday come, farewell, my dear!
  Hey derry down, down derry,
When we do meet we'll have good cheer,
  And then I will be merry:
If thou love me, I will love thee,
  And still delight in thy company,
                Thy company,
  Hey derry down, down derry.

from THE GENTLE CRAFT   *Thomas Deloney*

SONG

AND can the physician make sick men well?
  And can the magician a fortune divine?
Without lily, germander, and sops-in-wine,
        With sweet-briar
        And bon-fire
        And strawberry wire
        And columbine.

Within and out, in and out, round as a ball,
With hither and thither, as straight as a line,
With lily, germander, and sops-in-wine,
> *With sweet-briar*
> *And bon-fire*
> *And strawberry wire*
> *And columbine.*

When Saturn did live, there lived no poor,
The king and the beggar with roots did dine,
With lily, germander, and sops-in-wine,
> *With sweet-briar*
> *And bon-fire*
> *And strawberry wire*
> *And columbine.*

from ROBIN GOOD-FELLOW (*before* 1600)   *Anon.*

NATURAL COMPARISONS WITH PERFECT LOVE

THE lowest Trees have tops, the Ant her gall,
   The fly her spleen, the little sparks their heat:
The slender hairs cast shadows, though but small,
And Bees have stings, although they be not great:
   Seas have their source, and so have shallow springs,
   And love is love, in Beggars, as in Kings.

Where rivers smoothest run, deep are the fords,
The Dial stirs, yet none perceives it move:
The firmest faith is in the fewest words,
The Turtles cannot sing, and yet they love:
   True Hearts have eyes, and ears, no tongues to speak,
   They hear, and see, and sigh; and then they break.

from DAVISON'S POETICAL RHAPSODY (1602)   *Edward Dyer?*

47

SONG OF THE BEGGARS
IN PRAISE OF A BEGGAR'S LIFE

Bright shines the sun; play, beggars, play!
Here's scraps enough to serve to-day.

WHAT noise of viols is so sweet
  As when our merry clappers ring?
What mirth doth want where beggars meet?
  A beggar's life is for a king.
Eat, drink, and play; sleep when we list;
Go where we will, so stocks be missed.
    Bright shines the sun; play, beggars, play!
    Here's scraps enough to serve to-day.

The world is ours, and ours alone;
  For we alone have worlds at will;
We purchase not, all is our own;
  Both fields and streets we beggars fill.
Nor care to get, nor fear to keep,
Did ever break a beggar's sleep.
    Bright shines the sun; play, beggars, play!
    Here's scraps enough to serve to-day.

from A POETICAL RHAPSODY (1602)   *A. W.*

SISTER, AWAKE!

SISTER, awake! close not your eyes,
  The day her light discloses;
And the bright morning doth arise
  Out of her bed of roses.

See the clear sun, the world's bright eye,
  In at our window peeping;
Lo, how he blusheth to espy
  Us idle wenches sleeping!

48

Therefore awake, make haste I say,
And let us without staying
All in our gowns of green so gay
Into the park a-maying.

from BATESON'S ENGLISH MADRIGALS (1604)   *Anon.*

SONG OF THE FOX

TO-MORROW the fox will come to town,
   Keep, keep, keep, keep, keep,
To-morrow the fox will come to town,
   O keep you all well there,
I must desire you, neighbours all,
To hallo the fox out of the hall,
And cry as loud as you can call,
   Whoop, whoop, whoop, whoop, whoop.

He'll steal the Cock out from his flock,
   Keep, keep, keep, keep, keep,
He'll steal the Cock out from his flock,
   O keep you all well there.
I must desire you . . .

He'll steal the Hen out of the pen,
   Keep, keep, keep, keep, keep,
He'll steal the Hen out of the pen,
   O keep you all well there.
I must desire you . . .

He'll steal the Duck out of the brook,
   Keep, keep, keep, keep, keep,
He'll steal the Duck out of the brook,
   O keep you all well there.
I must desire you . . .

D   49

He'll steal the Lamb even from his dam,
Keep, keep, keep, keep, keep,
He'll steal the Lamb even from his dam,
O keep you all well there.
I must desire you, neighbours all,
To hallo the fox out of the hall,
And cry as loud as you can call,
Whoop, whoop, whoop, whoop, whoop.

from RAVENSCROFT'S DEUTEROMELIA (1609)　　　***Traditional***

A WOOING SONG
OF A YEOMAN OF KENT'S SON

ICH have house and land in Kent
　And if you'll love me, love me now,
Twopence-halfpenny is my rent,
　Ich cannot come every day to woo.
　　Chorus: Twopence-halfpenny is his rent,
　　　　　　　And he cannot come every day to woo.

Ich am my vather's eldest zonne,
　My mother eke doth love me well,
For ich can bravely clout my shoone,
　And ich full well can ring a bell.
　　Chorus: For he can bravely clout his shoone,
　　　　　　　And he full well can ring a bell.

My vather he gave me a hog,
　My mother she gave me a sow;
Ich have a God-vather dwells thereby,
　And he on me bestowed a plow.
　　Chorus: He has a God-vather dwells thereby,
　　　　　　　And he on him bestowed a plow.

One time ich gave thee a paper of pins,
　Another time a tawdry-lace;

50

And if thou wilt not grant me love,
   In truth ich die bevore thy face.
     Chorus : And if thou wilt not grant his love,
       In truth he'll die bevore thy face.

Ich have been twice our Whitson lord,
   Ich have had ladies many vair,
And eke thou hast my heart in hold
   And in my mind zeems passing rare.
     Chorus : And eke thou hast his heart in hold,
       And in his mind zeems passing rare.

Ich will put on my best white slops
   And ich will wear my yellow hose,
And on my head a good grey hat,
   And in't ich stick a yellow rose.
     Chorus : And on his head a good grey hat,
       And in't he'll stick a yellow rose.

Wherefore cease off, make no delay,
   And if you'll love me, love me now
Or else ich zeek zome oderwhere,
   For ich cannot come every day to woo.
     Chorus : Or else he'll zeek zome oderwhere,
       For he cannot come every day to woo.

from MELISMATA (1611)   *Traditional*

THE SPANISH ARMADA

*A Hymn to be sung by all England—women, youths, clerks
and soldiers*

FROM merciless invaders,
   From wicked men's device,—
O Lord! arise and help us
To quell our enemies.

Sink deep their potent navies,
Their strength and courage break:
O Lord! arise and save us,
For Jesus Christ his sake.

Though cruel Spain and Parma
With heathen legions come,
O God! arise and arm us—
For to defend our home.

We will not change our Bible
For Pope nor ban nor bell;
And if Apollyon come himself,
His fiery darts we'll quell.

John Still (1543–1608)

THE SHEPHERDS' BRAWL
ONE HALF ANSWERING THE OTHER

WE love, and have our love rewarded.
The others would answer:
We love, and are no whit regarded.
The first again:
We find most sweet affection's snare.
With like tune it should be as in a quire sent back again:
That sweet but sour despairful care.
A third time likewise thus:
Who can despair whom hope doth bear?
The answer:
And who can hope that feels despair?
Then all joyning their voyces, and dancing a faster measure, they would conclude with some such words:

As without breath no pipe doth move,
No music kindly without love.

Sir Philip Sidney (1554–1586)

DIRGE

FEAR no more the heat o' the sun,
   Nor the furious winter's rages;
Thou thy worldly task hast done,
   Home art gone, and ta'en thy wages:
Golden lads and girls all must,
As chimney-sweepers, come to dust.

Fear no more the frown o' the great;
   Thou art past the tyrant's stroke:
Care no more to clothe and eat;
   To thee the reed is as the oak:
The sceptre, learning, physic, must
All follow this, and come to dust.

Fear no more the lightning-flash,
   Nor the all-dreaded thunder-stone;
Fear not slander, censure rash;
   Thou hast finished joy and moan:
All lovers young, all lovers must
Consign to thee, and come to dust.

   No exorciser harm thee!
   Nor no witchcraft charm thee!
   Ghost unlaid forbear thee!
   Nothing ill come near thee!
   Quiet consummation have;
   And renownèd be thy grave!

from CYMBELINE   William Shakespeare (1564–1616)

SONG OF VER AND HIS TRAIN
(overlaid with suits of green moss, representing short grass)

SPRING, the sweet Spring, is the year's pleasant king;
Then blooms each thing, then maids dance in a ring,
Cold doth not sting, the pretty birds do sing,
    Cuckoo, jug-jug, pu-we, to-witta-woo!

The palm and may make country houses gay,
Lambs frisk and play, the shepherds pipe all day,
And we hear aye birds tune this merry lay,
    Cuckoo, jug-jug, pu-we, to-witta-woo!

The fields breathe sweet, the daisies kiss our feet,
Young lovers meet, old wives a-sunning sit,
In every street these tunes our ears do greet,
    Cuckoo, jug-jug, pu-we, to-witta-woo!
      Spring! the sweet Spring!

DIRGE OF THE SATYRS AND WOOD-NYMPHS AS THEY CARRY OUT THE DEAD SUMMER

AUTUMN hath all the summer's fruitful treasure;
Gone is our sport, fled is poor Croydon's[1] pleasure!
Short days, sharp days, long nights come on apace:
Ah, who shall hide us from the winter's face?
Cold doth increase, the sickness will not cease,
And here we lie, God knows, with little ease.
    From winter, plague, and pestilence, good Lord, deliver us!
London doth mourn, Lambeth is quite forlorn!
Trades cry, woe worth that ever they were born!

            [1] Corydon

The want of term is town and city's harm;
Close chambers we do want to keep us warm.
Long banishëd must we live from our friends:
This low-built house will bring us to our ends.
   From winter, plague, and pestilence, good Lord, deliver us!
from SUMMER'S LAST WILL AND TESTAMENT
                       Thomas Nashe (1567–1601)

A HYMN IN PRAISE OF NEPTUNE

OF Neptune's empire let us sing,
   At whose command the waves obey;
  To whom the rivers tribute pay,
Down the high mountains sliding;
  To whom the scaly nation yields
  Homage for the crystal fields
   Wherein they dwell;
And every sea-god pays a gem
  Yearly out of his wat'ry cell,
To deck great Neptune's diadem.

The Tritons dancing in a ring,
  Before his palace gates do make
  The water with their echoes quake,
Like the great thunder sounding:
  The sea nymphs chant their accents shrill,
  And the Syrens taught to kill
   With their sweet voice,
Make every echoing rock reply,
   Unto their gentle murmuring noise,
The praise of Neptune's empery.

             Thomas Campion (1567–1619)

NOW WINTER NIGHTS ENLARGE

NOW winter nights enlarge
    The number of their hours,
And clouds their storms discharge
Upon the airy towers.
Let now the chimneys blaze,
And cups o'erflow with wine;
Let well-tuned words amaze
With harmony divine.
Now yellow waxen lights
Shall wait on honey love,
While youthful revels, masques, and courtly sights
Sleep's leaden spells remove.

This time doth well dispense
With lovers' long discourse;
Much speech hath some defence,
Though beauty no remorse.
All do not all things well;
Some measures comely tread,
Some knotted riddles tell,
Some poems smoothly read.
The summer hath his joys
And winter his delights;
Though love and all his pleasures are but toys,
They shorten tedious nights.

from THE THIRD BOOK OF AIRS (*c.* 1617)   *Thomas Campion*

A PALINODE

AS withereth the primrose by the river,
    As fadeth summer's sun from gliding fountains,
As vanisheth the light-blown bubble ever,
As melteth snow upon the mossy mountains:
56

So melts, so vanisheth, so fades, so withers
The rose, the shine, the bubble and the snow,
Of praise, pomp, glory, joy, which short life gathers,
Fair praise, vain pomp, sweet glory, brittle joy.
The withered primrose by the mourning river,
The faded summer's sun from weeping fountains,
The light-blown bubble, vanishëd for ever,
The molten snow upon the naked mountains,
    Are emblems that the treasures we up-lay,
    Soon wither, vanish, fade, and melt away.

For as the snow, whose lawn did overspread
Th' ambitious hills, which giant-like did threat
To pierce the heaven with their aspiring head,
Naked and bare doth leave their craggy seat:
Whenas the bubble, which did empty fly
The dalliance of the undiscernëd wind,
On whose calm rolling waves it did rely,
Hath shipwreck made, where it did dalliance find:
And when the sunshine which dissolved the snow,
Coloured the bubble with a pleasant vary,
And made the rathe and timely primrose grow,
Swarth clouds withdraw, which longer time do tarry:
    O what is praise, pomp, glory, joy, but so
    As shine by fountains, bubbles, flowers or snow?

from ENGLAND'S HELICON   *Edmund Bolton* (1575–1633)

SONG OF CERES, PROSERPINE, SWAINS AND COUNTRY WENCHES

WITH fair Ceres, Queen of grain.
    The reapëd fields we roam, roam, roam,
Each Country Peasant, Nymph, and Swain,
Sing their harvest home, home, home:
    Whilst the Queen of Plenty hallows
    Growing fields as well as fallows.

Echo double all our Lays,
Make the Champians sound, sound, sound
To the Queen of Harvest praise,
That sows and reaps our ground, ground, ground—
   Ceres, Queen of plenty, hallows
   Growing fields as well as fallows.

Tempests hence, hence winds and hails,
Tares, cockles, rotten showers, showers, showers,
Our song shall keep time with our flails,
When Ceres sings, none lowers, lowers, lowers.
   She it is whose God-hood hallows
   Growing fields as well as fallows.

from THE SILVER AGE   *Thomas Heywood* (1573?–1641)

THE CRIES OF ROME

   Thus go the cries in Rome's fair town,
   First they go up street, and then they go down.

ROUND and sound all of a colour
   Buy a very fine marking stone, marking stone,
Round and sound all of a colour,
Buy a very fine marking stone, a very very fine.
   Thus go, etc.
Bread and—meat—bread—and meat
For the—ten—der—mercy of God to the
poor pris—ners of Newgate four—
score and ten—poor—prisoners—
   Thus go, etc.
Salt—salt—white Wor—stershire salt,
   Thus go, etc.

Buy a very fine Mouse-trap or a tormentor
for your Fleas.
Thus go, etc.
Kitchen—stuffe maids,
Thus go, etc.
Ha' ye any Wood to clear?
Thus go, etc.
I ha' white Radish, white
hard Lettuce, white young Onions—
Thus go, etc.
I ha' Rock-sampier, Rock-sampier—
Thus go, etc.
Buy a Mat, a Mil-mat,
Mat, or a Hassock for your pew,
A stopple for your close stool,
Or a Pesock to thrust your feet in—
Thus go, etc.
Whiting maids Whiting
Thus go, etc.
Hot fine Oat-cakes, hot—
Thus go, etc.
Small Coals here.
Thus go, etc.
Will you buy any Milk to-day?
Thus go, etc.
Lanthorn and candlelight here,
Maid, a light here—
Thus go the cries in Rome's fair town,
First they go up street, and then they go down.

from THE RAPE OF LUCRECE   *Thomas Heywood*

I

MARRIAGE SONG

ROSES, their sharp spines being gone,
　Not royal in their smells alone,
　But in their hue;
Maiden pinks, of odour faint,
Daisies smell-less, yet most quaint,
　And sweet thyme true;

Primrose, first-born child of Ver,
Merry spring-time's harbinger,
　With her bells dim:
Oxlips in their cradles growing,
Marigolds on death-beds blowing,
　Lark's-heels trim;

All, dear Nature's children sweet,
Lie 'fore bride and bridegroom's feet,
　Blessing their sense!
Not an angel of the air,
Bird melodious or bird fair,
　Be absent hence!

The crow, the slanderous cuckoo, nor
The boding raven, nor chough hoar,
　Nor chatt'ring pie,
May on our bridehouse perch or sing,
Or with them any discord bring,
　But from it fly!

II

FUNERAL SONG

URNS and odours bring away,
  Vapors, sighs, darken the day!
Our dole more deadly looks than dying!
  Balms, and gums, and heavy cheers,
  Sacred vials fill'd with tears,
And clamours, through the wild air flying:

  Come, all sad and solemn shows,
  That are quick-eyed Pleasure's foes!
  We convent nought else but woes:
  We convent nought else but woes.

from THE TWO NOBLE KINSMEN   *John Fletcher* (1579–1625)

SONGS OF THE SHEPHERDS

I

SING his praises that doth keep
  Our flocks from harm,
Pan, the father of our sheep;
    And arm in arm
Tread we softly in a round,
While the hollow neighb'ring ground
Fills the music with her sound.

Pan, oh, great god Pan, to thee
    Thus do we sing:
Thou that keep'st us chaste and free,
    As the young spring,
Ever be thy honour spoke,
From that place the morn is broke,
To that place day doth unyoke!

All ye woods, and trees, and bowers,
All ye virtues and ye powers
That inhabit in the lakes,
In the pleasant springs or brakes,
　　Move your feet
　　　　To our sound,
　　Whilst we greet
　　　　All this ground
With his honour and his name
That defends our flocks from blame.

He is great, and he is just,
He is ever good, and must
Thus be honour'd. Daffadillies,
Roses, pinks, and lovèd lilies,
　　Let us fling,
　　Whilst we sing,
　　Ever holy,
　　Ever holy,
Ever honour'd, ever young!
Thus great Pan is ever sung!

from THE FAITHFUL SHEPHERDESS　　　　　　*John Fletcher*

SONG FOR THE SICK EMPEROR

CARE-CHARMING Sleep, thou easer of all woes,
　Brother to Death, sweetly thyself dispose
On this afflicted prince; fall like a cloud,
In gentle showers; give nothing that is loud,
Or painful to his slumbers; easy, sweet,
And as a purling stream, thou son of Night,

Pass by his troubled senses, sing his pain,
Like hollow murmuring wind, or silver rain.
Into this prince gently, oh, gently slide,
And kiss him into slumbers like a bride!

from VALENTINIAN   *John Fletcher*

BATTLE SONG

ARM, arm, arm, arm! the scouts are all come in.
   Keep your ranks close, and now your honours win.
Behold from yonder hill the foe appears;
Bows, bills, glaves, arrows, shields, and spears;
Like a dark wood he comes, or tempest pouring;
Oh, view the wings of horse the meadows scouring!
The van-guard marches bravely. Hark, the drums,
         Dub, dub!
They meet, they meet! Now the battle comes:
   See how the arrows fly,
   That darken all the sky;
   Hark how the trumpets sound,
   Hark how the hills rebound!
         Tara, tara, tara, tara, tara!
Hark how the horses charge! In, boys, boys, in!
The battle totters; now the wounds begin;
     Oh, how they cry,
     Oh, how they die!
Room for the valiant Memnon arm'd with thunder!
   See how he breaks the ranks asunder.
They fly, they fly! Eumenes has the chase,
And brave Polybius makes good his place.
   To the plains, to the woods,
   To the rocks, to the floods,
  They fly for succour. Follow, follow, follow!
  Hark how the soldiers hollo!

Hey, *hey*,
Brave Diocles is dead,
And all his soldiers fled,
The battle's won, and lost,
That many a life has cost.

from THE MAD LOVER   *John Fletcher*

SONG OF THE SIRENS

STEER hither, steer your wingëd pines,
  All beaten mariners!
Here lie Love's undiscovered mines,
  A prey to passengers;
Perfumes far sweeter than the best
Which make the Phœnix' urn and nest.
      Fear not your ships,
Nor any to oppose you save our lips;
      But come on shore
Where no joy dies till love hath gotten more.

For swelling waves, our panting breasts
  Where never storms arise,
Exchange; and be awhile our guests:
  For stars, gaze on our eyes.
The compass Love shall hourly sing,
And as he goes about the ring,
      We will not miss
To tell each point he nameth with a kiss.
      Then come on shore,
Where no joy dies till love hath gotten more.

from THE INNER TEMPLE MASQUE
                    William Browne (1591–1643)

FUNERAL SONG

WHILST we sing the doleful knell
    Of this princess' passing-bell,
Let the woods and valleys ring
Echoes to our sorrowing;
And the tenor of their song
Be ding dong, ding dong, dong,
    Ding dong, dong,
        Ding dong.

Nature now shall boast no more
Of the riches of her store,
Since in this her chiefest prize
All the stock of beauty dies:
Then what cruel heart can long
Forbear to sing this sad ding dong?
    This sad ding dong,
        Ding dong.

Fauns and sylvans of the woods,
Nymphs that haunt the crystal floods,
Savage beasts more milder then
The unrelenting hearts of men,
Be partakers of our moan,
And with us sing ding dong, ding dong,
    Ding dong, dong,
        Ding dong.

from SWETNAM, THE WOMAN-HATER   *Anonymous* (1620)

THE LAMENT OF DAVID AND
THE PEOPLE OF ISRAEL FOR
SAUL AND JONATHAN

THE beauty of Israel is slain upon thy high places:
>   *How are the mighty fallen!*
Tell it not in Gath,
Publish it not in the streets of Askelon;
>   Lest the daughters of the Philistines rejoice,
>   Lest the daughters of the uncircumcised triumph.
Ye mountains of Gilboa, let there be no dew,
Neither let there be rain, upon you, nor fields of offerings:
>   For there the shield of the mighty is vilely cast away,
>   The shield of Saul, as though he had not been anointed
>   with oil.
From the blood of the slain,
From the fat of the mighty,
>   The bow of Jonathan turned not back,
>   And the sword of Saul returned not empty.
Saul and Jonathan were lovely and pleasant in their lives,
And in their death they were not divided:
>   They were swifter than eagles,
>   They were stronger than lions.
Ye daughters of Israel,
Weep over Saul,
>   Who clothed you in scarlet with other delights,
>   Who put on ornaments of gold upon your apparel.
>   *How are the mighty fallen in the midst of the battle!*
O Jonathan, thou wast slain in thine high places.
I am distressed for thee, my brother Jonathan:

66

Very pleasant hast thou been unto me:
Thy love to me was wonderful,
Passing the love of women.
How are the mighty fallen,
And the weapons of war perished!

2 Samuel I. 19-27

PSALM XLVI

GOD is our refuge and strength,
A very present help in trouble.
Therefore will not we fear, though the earth be removed,
 And though the mountains be carried into the midst of
  the sea;
Though the waters thereof roar and be troubled,
 Though the mountains shake with the swelling thereof.
There is a river, the streams whereof shall make glad the
  city of God,
 The holy place of the tabernacles of the most High.
God is in the midst of her, she shall not be moved:
 God shall help her, and that right early.
The heathen raged, the kingdoms were moved:
 He uttered his voice, the earth melted.
  The Lord of Hosts is with us;
  The God of Jacob is our refuge.
Come, behold the works of the Lord,
 What desolations he hath made in the earth.
He maketh wars to cease unto the end of the earth;
 He breaketh the bow, and cutteth the spear in sunder;
 He burneth the chariot in the fire.
Be still, and know that I am God:
 I will be exalted among the heathen,
I will be exalted in the earth.
  The Lord of Hosts is with us;
  The God of Jacob is our refuge.

PSALM CXXVI

WHEN the Lord turned again the captivity of Sion,
We were like them that dream.
Then was our mouth filled with laughter,
And our tongue with singing:
Then said they among the heathen,
The Lord hath done great things for them.
The Lord hath done great things for us,
Whereof we are glad.
Turn again our captivity, O Lord,
As the streams in the south.
They that sow in tears
Shall reap in joy.
He that goeth forth and weepeth,
Bearing precious seed,
Shall doubtless come again with rejoicing,
Bringing his sheaves with him.

PSALM CL

Praise ye the Lord.

PRAISE God in his sanctuary:
Praise him in the firmament of his power.
Praise him for his mighty acts:
Praise him according to his excellent greatness.
Praise him with the sound of the trumpet:
Praise him with the psaltery and harp.
Praise him with the timbrel and dance:
Praise him with stringed instruments and organs.
Praise him with the loud cymbals:
Praise him with the high-sounding cymbals.
Let everything that hath breath praise the Lord.

Praise ye the Lord.

From *ISAIAH*

AND there shall come forth a rod out of the stem of
Jesse,
And a Branch shall grow out of his roots:
And the spirit of the Lord shall rest upon him,
 The spirit of wisdom and understanding,
 The spirit of counsel and might,
 The spirit of knowledge and of the fear of the Lord;
And shall make him of quick understanding in the fear of
  the Lord:
And he shall not judge after the sight of his eyes,
 Neither reprove after the hearing of his ears:
But with righteousness shall he judge the poor,
 And reprove with equity for the meek of the earth:
And he shall strike the earth with the rod of his mouth,
 And with the breath of his lips shall he slay the wicked.
And righteousness shall be the girdle of his loins,
 And faithfulness the girdle of his reins.
The wolf also shall dwell with the lamb,
 And the leopard shall lie down with the kid;
And the calf and the young lion and the fatling together;
And a little child shall lead them.
And the cow and the bear shall feed;
 Their young ones shall lie down together:
And the lion shall eat straw like the ox.
And the sucking child shall play on the hole of the asp,
 And the weaned child shall put his hand on the cocka-
  trice' den.
They shall not hurt nor destroy in all my holy mountain:
For the earth shall be full of the knowledge of the Lord,
 As the waters cover the sea.
And in that day there shall be a root of Jesse,
 Which shall stand for an ensign of the people;
To it shall the Gentiles seek:
 And his rest shall be glorious.   *Isaiah* XI. 1–10

From *THE WISDOM OF SOLOMON*

THE souls of the righteous are in the hand of God,
And there shall no torment touch them.
In the sight of the unwise they seemed to die:
And their departure is taken for misery,
And their going from us to be utter destruction:
But they are in peace.
For though they be punished in the sight of men,
Yet is their hope full of immortality.
And having been a little chastised,
They shall be greatly rewarded:
For God proved them,
And found them worthy of himself.
As gold in the furnace hath he tried them,
And received them as a burnt offering.
And in the time of their visitation they shall shine,
And run to and fro as sparks among the stubble.
They shall judge the nations,
And have dominion over the people,
And their Lord shall reign for ever.
They that put their trust in him shall understand the truth:
And such as be faithful in love shall abide with him:
For grace and mercy is to his saints,
And he hath care for his elect.
For glorious is the fruit of good labours;
And the root of wisdom shall never fall away.

Wisdom of Solomon, III. 1–8, 15

From *ECCLESIASTICUS*

I

HE hath garnished the excellent works of his wisdom,
And he is from everlasting to everlasting: . . .

The pride of the height, the clear firmament,
The beauty of heaven, with his glorious shew;
The sun when it appeareth, declaring at his rising a marvellous instrument,
The work of the most High: . . .
Great is the Lord that made it;
And at his commandment it runneth hastily.
He made the moon also to serve in her season for a declaration of times,
And a sign of the world . . .
The month is called after her name, increasing wonderfully in her changing,
Being an instrument of the armies above, shining in the firmament of heaven;
The beauty of heaven, the glory of the stars,
An ornament giving light in the highest places of the Lord.
At the commandment of the Holy One they will stand in their order,
And never faint in their watches.
Look upon the rainbow, and praise him that made it;
Very beautiful it is in the brightness thereof.
It compasseth the heaven about with a glorious circle,
And the hands of the Most High have bended it.
By his commandment he maketh the snow to fall apace,
And sendeth swiftly the lightnings of his judgment.
Through this the treasures are opened:
And clouds fly forth as fowls.
By his great power he maketh the clouds firm,
And the hailstones are broken small.
At his sight the mountains are shaken,
And at his will the south wind bloweth.
The noise of the thunder maketh the earth to tremble:
So doth the northern storm and the whirlwind:
As birds flying he scattereth the snow,

And the falling down thereof is as the lighting of grass-
hoppers:
The eye marvelleth at the beauty of the whiteness thereof,
And the heart is astonished at the raining of it.
The hoar frost also as salt he poureth on the earth,
And being congealed, it lieth on the top of sharp stakes.
When the cold north wind bloweth, and the water is con-
gealed into ice,
It abideth upon every gathering together of water,
And clotheth the water as with a breastplate. . . .

We may speak much, and yet come short:
Wherefore in sum, he is all.

Ecclesiasticus, XLII. 21; XLIII. 1, 2, 5, 6, 8–20, 27

II

LET us now praise famous men,
And our fathers that begat us.
The Lord hath wrought great glory by them through his
great power from the beginning.
Such as did bear rule in their kingdoms, men renowned for
their power,
Giving counsel by their understanding, and declaring pro-
phecies:
Leaders of the people by their counsels,
And by their knowledge of learning meet for the people,
Wise and eloquent in their instructions:
Such as found out musical tunes,
And recited verses in writing:
Rich men furnished with ability, living peaceably in their
habitations:
All these were honoured in their generations,
And were the glory of their times.
There be of them that have left a name behind them,
That their praises might be reported.

And some there be, which have no memorial;
Who are perished, as though they had never been;
And are become as though they had never been born;
And their children after them.
But these were merciful men,
Whose righteousness hath not been forgotten.
With their seed shall continually remain a good inheritance,
And their children are within the covenant.
Their seed standeth fast,
And their children for their sakes.
Their seed shall remain for ever,
And their glory shall not be blotted out.
Their bodies are buried in peace;
But their name liveth for evermore.

Ecclesiasticus, XLIV. 1–14

William Drummond of Hawthornden
1585–1649

FOR THE NATIVITY OF OUR LORD

The Angels

RUN, shepherds, run where Bethlem blest appears,
We bring the best of news, be not dismayed,
A Saviour there is born, more old than years,
Amidst heaven's rolling heights this earth who stayed.
In a poor cottage inned, a virgin maid
A weakling did him bear, who all upbears:
There is he poorly swaddled, in manger laid,
To whom too narrow swaddlings are our spheres:
Run, shepherds, run, and solemnize his birth,
This is that night—no, day, grown great with bliss,

In which the power of Satan broken is;
In heaven be glory, peace unto the earth!
  Thus singing, through the air the angels swam,
  And cope of stars re-echoèd the same.

The Shepherds

O than the fairest day thrice fairer night!
Night to best days in which a sun doth rise,
Of which that golden eye, which clears the skies,
Is but a sparkling ray, a shadow light:
And blessed ye, in silly-pastors' sight,
Mild creatures, in whose warm crib now lies
That heaven-sent youngling, holy-maid-born wight,
'Midst, end, beginning of our prophecies:
Blest cottage that hath flowers in winter spread;
Though withered, blessed grass, that hath the grace
To deck and be a carpet to that place.
Thus sang, unto the sounds of oaten reed,
  Before the babe, the shepherds bowed on knees,
  And springs ran nectar, honey dropt from trees.

Alexander Montgomerie

1556?–1610?

THE NIGHT IS NEIR GONE

HAY! now the day dawis;
  The jolly Cock crawis;
Now shroudis the shawis[1]
  Through Nature anon.

[1] *Now shroudis the shawis* = now the thickets clothe themselves

The thissell-cock cryis
On lovers who lyis,
Now skaillis[1] the skyis:
     The night is neir gone.

The feildis overflowis
With gowans that growis,
Where lilies like low[2] is,
     As red as the rone.[3]
The turtle that true is,
With notes that renewis,
Her pairtie[4] pursewis;
     The night is neir gone.

Now hairtis with hindis
Conforme to their kindis
High tosses their tyndis[5]
     On ground where they grone.
Now hurchonis[6] with hairis
Ay passis in pairis;
Which duly declairis
     The night is neir gone.

The season excellis
Through sweetness that smellis;
Now Cupid compellis
     Our heartis echone
On Venus who waikis,
To muse on our maikis,[7]
Syn[8] sing for their saikis—
     The night is neir gone.

[1] clear
[4] mate
[7] mates

[2] flame
[5] antlers
[8] then

[3] rowan
[6] hedge-hogs

All curageous knichtis
Aganes the day dichtis[1]
The breast-plate that bright is
  To fight with their fone.
The stoned steed[2] stampis
Through courage and crampis,[3]
Syn on the land lampis.[4]
  The night is neir gone.

The freikis[5] on feildis,
That wight[6] wapins weildis,
With shining bright sheildis,
  As Titan in trone;
Stiff speiris in restis
Over coursoris crestis
Are broke on their breistis:
  The night is neir gone.

So hard are their hittis,
Some swayis, some sittis,
And some perforce flittis
  On ground while they grone.
Syn groomis that gay is
On blonkis[7] that brayis
With swordis assayis:
  The night is neir gone.

---

[1] prepare   [2] *stoned steed* = stallion   [3] prances
[4] gallops   [5] warriors   [6] strong
[7] white horses

Michael Drayton

1563–1631

TO THE VIRGINIAN VOYAGE

YOU brave heroic minds,
　　Worthy your country's name;
　That honour still pursue,
　Go, and subdue,
Whilst loitering hinds
Lurk here at home, with shame.

Britons, you stay too long,
Quickly aboard bestow you,
　And with a merry gale,
　Swell your stretched sail,
With vows as strong
As the winds that blow you.

Your course securely steer,
West and by south forth keep,
　Rocks, lee-shores, nor shoals,
　When Aeolus scowls,
You need not fear,
So absolute the deep.

And cheerfully at sea
Success you still entice,
　To get the pearl and gold,
　And ours to hold
Virginia,
Earth's only Paradise.

77

Where Nature hath in store
Fowl, venison, and fish,
  And the fruitfullest soil,
  Without your toil,
Three harvests more,
All greater than your wish.

And the ambitious vine
Crowns with his purple mass
  The cedar reaching high
  To kiss the sky,
The cypress, pine
And useful sassafras.

To whom the Golden Age
Still Nature's laws doth give,
  No other cares that tend,
  But them to defend
From winter's rage,
That long there doth not live.

When as the luscious smell
Of that delicious land,
  Above the seas that flows,
  The clear wind throws,
Your hearts to swell
Approaching the dear strand;

In kenning of the shore
(Thanks to God first given)
  O you the happiest men
  Be frolic then,
Let cannons roar
Frighting the wide heaven.

And in regions far
Such heroes bring ye forth,
　　As those from whom we came,
　　And plant our name,
Under that star
Not known unto our North.

And as there plenty grows
Of laurel everywhere,
　　Apollo's sacred tree,
　　You may it see,
A poet's brows
To crown, that may sing there.

Thy voyages attend,
Industrious Hackluyt,
　　Whose reading shall inflame
　　Men to seek fame,
And much commend
To after-times thy wit.

Henry King
1592–1669
William Browne
1588–1643

Simon Wastell
fl. 1629
William Strode
1600–1645

SIC VITA

1

LIKE to the falling of a star;
　Or as the flights of eagles are;
Or like the fresh spring's gaudy hue;
Or silver drops of morning dew:
Or like a wind that chafes the flood;

Or bubbles on the water stood;
Even such is man, whose borrow'd light
Is straight call'd in, and paid to night.
   The wind blows out; the bubble dies;
   The Spring entombed in Autumn lies;
   The dew dries up; the star is shot;
   The flight is past; and man forgot.

Henry King

II

Like to the Grass that's newly sprung;
Or like a tale that's new begun;
Or like the bird that's here to-day;
Or like the pearlèd dew of May;
Or like an hour; or like a span;
Or like the singing of a swan;
Even such is man, who lives by breath,
Is here, now there, in life, and death.
   The grass withers; the tale is ended;
   The bird is flown; the dew's ascended;
   The hour is short; the span not long;
   The swan's near death; man's life is done.

Simon Wastell

III

Like to a silkworm of one year;
Or like a wrongèd lover's tear;
Or on the waves a rudder's dint;
Or like the sparkles of a glint;
Or like to little cakes perfum'd;
Or fireworks made to be consum'd;
Even such is man, and all that trust
In weak and animated dust.

The silkworm droops; the tears soon shed;
The ship's way lost; the sparkle dead;
The cake is burnt; the fire-work done;
And man as these as quickly gone.

William Browne

IV

Like to the rolling of an eye;
Or like a star shot from the sky;
Or like a hand upon a clock;
Or like a wave upon a rock;
Or like a wind; or like a flame;
Or like false news which people frame;
Even such is man, of equal stay
Whose very growth leads to decay.
   The eye is turned; the star down bendeth;
   The hand doth steal; the wave descendeth;
   The wind is spent; the flame unfir'd;
   The news disprov'd; man's life expir'd.

V

Like to an eye which sleep doth chain;
Or like a star whose fall we feign;
Or like a shade on Ahaz' watch;
Or like a wave which gulfs do snatch;
Or like a wind or flame that's past;
Or smother'd news confirm'd at last;
Even so man's life, pawn'd in the grave,
Waits for a rising it must have.
   The eye still sees; the star still blazeth;
   The shade goes back; the wave escapeth;
   The wind is turn'd, the flame reviv'd;
   The news renew'd; and man new liv'd.

William Strode

F

George Herbert
1593-1633

ANTIPHONS

I

Chor.] LET all the world in every corner sing,
            My God and King.

Ver.]   The heavens are not too high,
      His praise may thither fly:
      The earth is not too low,
      His praises there may grow.

Chor.] Let all the world in every corner sing,
            My God and King.

Ver.]   The Church with Psalms must shout,
      No door can keep them out:
      But above all, the heart
      Must bear the longest part.

Chor.] Let all the world in every corner sing,
            My God and King.

II

Chor.] Praised be the God of love,
Men]   Here below,
Angels] And here above:

Chor.] Who hath dealt his mercies so,
Ang.]   To his friend,
Men]   And to his foe;

Chor.] That both grace and glory tend
Ang.]   Us of old,
Men]   And us in the end.

Chor.]　The great Shepherd of the fold
Ang.]　　Us did make,
Men]　　For us was sold.

Chor.]　He our foes in pieces brake:
Ang.]　　Him we touch;
Men]　　And him we take.

Chor.]　Wherefore since that he is such,
Ang.]　　We adore,
Men]　　And we do crouch.

Chor.]　Lord, thy praises shall be more.
Men]　　We have none,
Ang.]　　And we no store.

Chor.]　Praisèd be the God alone
　　　　Who hath made of two folds one.

HEAVEN

Echo]　O WHO will show me those delights on high?
　　　　　　　　　　　　　　　　　　　I.
Thou Echo, thou art mortal, all men know.
　　　　　　　　　　　　　　　No.
Wert thou not born among the trees and leaves?
　　　　　　　　　　　　　　Leaves.
And are there any leaves, that still abide?
　　　　　　　　　　　　　　Bide.
What leaves are they? impart the matter wholly.
　　　　　　　　　　　　　　Holy.
Are holy leaves the Echo then of bliss?
　　　　　　　　　　　　　　Yes.

83

Then tell me, what is that supreme delight?
> *Light.*

Light to the mind: what shall the will enjoy?
> *Joy.*

But are there cares and business with the pleasure?
> *Leisure.*

Light, joy, and leisure; but shall they persèver?
> *Ever.*

John Chalkhill

17th cent.

SONG

OH, the sweet contentment
The countryman doth find.
High trolollie lollie loe,
High trolollie lie,
That quiet contemplation
Possesseth all my mind:
> *Then care away,*
> *And wend along with me.*

For courts are full of flattery,
As hath too oft been tried;
> *High, etc.*
The city full of wantonness,
And both are full of pride.
> *Then, etc.*

But oh, the honest countryman
Speaks truly from his heart,
> *High, etc.*
His pride is in his tillage,
His horses and his cart,
> *Then, etc.*

Our clothing is good sheepskins,
Grey russet for our wives,
High, etc.
'Tis warmth and not gay clothing
That doth prolong our lives;
Then, etc.

The ploughman, though he labour hard,
Yet on his holiday,
High, etc.
No emperor so merrily
Does pass his time away;
Then, etc.

To recompense our tillage,
The heavens afford us showers;
High, etc.
And for our sweet refreshments
The earth affords us bowers:
Then, etc.

The cuckoo and the nightingale
Full merrily do sing,
High trolollie lollie loe,
High trolollie lie,
And with their pleasant roundelays
Bid welcome to the spring.
Then care away,
And wend along with me.

OH, THE BRAVE FISHER'S LIFE

OH, the brave fisher's life,
It is the best of any.
'Tis full of pleasure, void of strife,
And 'tis beloved of many:

Other joys
Are but toys,
Only this
Lawful is,
For our skill
Breeds no ill,
But content and pleasure.

In a morning up we rise
Ere Aurora's peeping,
Drink a cup to wash our eyes,
Leave the sluggards sleeping;
Then we go
To and fro,
With our knacks
At our backs,
To such streams
As the Thames,
If we have the leisure.

When we please to walk abroad
For our recreation,
In the fields is our abode,
Full of delectation:
Where in a brook
With a hook,
Or a lake
Fish we take,
There we sit
For a bit
Till we fish entangle.

We have gentles in a horn,
We have paste and worms too,

We can watch both night and morn,
Suffer rain and storms too:
    None do here
    Use to swear,
    Oaths do fray
    Fish away,
    We sit still,
    Watch our quill,
Fishers must not wrangle.

If the sun's excessive heat
Makes our bodies swelter,
To an osier hedge we get
For a friendly shelter,
    Where in a dike
    Perch or pike,
    Roach or dace
    We do chase,
    Bleak or gudgeon
    Without grudging,
We are still contented.

Or we sometimes pass an hour
Under a green willow,
That defends us from a shower,
Making earth our pillow;
    There we may
    Think and pray
    Before death
    Stops our breath;
    Other joys
    Are but toys
And to be lamented.

from THE ANGLER

George Wither

fl. 1622

A CHRISTMAS CAROL

So, now is come our joyfullest feast;
    Let every man be jolly.
Each room with ivy leaves is dressed,
    And every post with holly.
Though some churls at our mirth repine,
Round your foreheads garlands twine;
Drown sorrow in a cup of wine,
    And let us all be merry.

Now all our neighbours' chimneys smoke,
    And Christmas blocks are burning;
Their ovens they with baked meats choke,
    And all their spits are turning.
Without the door let sorrow lie;
And if for cold it hap to die,
We'll bury't in a Christmas pie,
    And evermore be merry.

Now every lad is wondrous trim,
    And no man minds his labour;
Our lasses have provided them
    A bagpipe and a tabor;
Young men and maids, and girls and boys,
Give life to one another's joys;
And you anon shall by their noise
    Perceive that they are merry.

Rank misers now do sparing shun;
    Their hall of music soundeth;
And dogs thence with whole shoulders run,
    So all things there aboundeth.
The country folks themselves advance
With crowdy-muttons out of France;
And Jack shall pipe and Jill shall dance,
    And all the town be merry.

Ned Squash hath fetched his bands from pawn,
    And all his best apparel;
Brisk Nell hath bought a ruff of lawn
    With droppings of the barrel;
And those that hardly all the year
Had bread to eat, or rags to wear,
Will have both clothes and dainty fare,
    And all the day be merry!

Now poor men to the justices
    With capons make their errands;
And if they hap to fail of these,
    They plague them with their warrants;
But now they feed them with good cheer,
And what they want they take in beer;
For Christmas comes but once a year,
    And then they shall be merry.

Good farmers in the country nurse
    The poor, that else were undone;
Some landlords spend their money worse
    On lust and pride at London.
There the roysters they do play,
Drab and dice their lands away,
Which may be ours another day;
    And therefore let's be merry.

The client now his suit forbears,
    The prisoner's heart is easèd;
The debtor drinks away his cares,
    And for the time is pleased.
Though other purses be more fat,
Why should we pine or grieve at that?
Hang sorrow! care will kill a cat,
    And therefore let's be merry.

Hark! how the wags abroad do call
    Each other forth to rambling;
Anon you'll see them in the hall
    For nuts and apples scrambling.
Hark! how the roofs with laughters sound!
Anon they'll think the house goes round,
For they the cellar's depth have found,
    And there they will be merry.

The wenches with their wassel-bowls
    About the streets are singing;
The boys are come to catch the owls,
    The wild mare is in bringing.
Our kitchen boy hath broke his box,
And to the dealing of the ox
Our honest neighbours come by flocks,
    And here they will be merry.

Now kings and queens poor sheep cots have,
    And mate with everybody;
The honest now may have the knave,
    And wise men play at noddy.
Some youths will now a-mumming go,
Some others play at Rowland-ho,
And twenty other gameboys mo,
    Because they will be merry.

Then wherefore in these merry days
  Should we, I pray, be duller?
No, let us sing some roundelays,
  To make our mirth the fuller.
And whilst thus inspired we sing,
Let all the streets with echoes ring,
Woods, and hills, and everything,
  Bear witness we are merry.

Jasper Fisher
fl. 1639

SONG

A T the spring
  Birds do sing:
Now with high,
Then low cry:
Flat, acute;
And salute
The Sun, born
Every morn.
[*All*] *He's no bard, that cannot sing*
  The praises of the flow'ry spring.

Flora queen,
All in green,
Doth delight
To paint white,
And to spread
Cruel red,
With a blue,
Colour true.
    He's no bard, etc.

Woods renew
Hunter's hue,
Shepherd's grey
Crowned with bay,
With his pipe
Care doth wipe,
Till he dream
By the stream.
  He's no bard, etc.

Faithful loves,
Turtle doves
Sit and bill
On a hill.
Country swains,
On the plains,
Run and leap,
Turn and skip.
  He's no bard, etc.

Pan doth play
Care away.
Fairies small
Two foot tall,
With caps red
On their head,
Dance a round
On the ground.
  He's no bard, etc.

from FUIMUS TROES

A MORISCO[1]

THE sky is glad that stars above
   Do give a brighter splendour:
The stars unfold their flaming gold,
   To make the ground more tender:
The ground doth send a fragrant smell,
   That air may be the sweeter:
The air doth charm the swelling seas
   With pretty chirping metre:
The sea with river's water doth
   Feed plants and flowers dainty:
The plants do yield their fruitful seed,
   That beasts may live in plenty:
The beasts do give both food and cloth,
   That men high Jove may honour;
And so the world runs merrily round,
   When peace doth smile upon her.
Oh then, then oh: oh then, then oh:
   This jubilee last for ever!
That foreign spite or civil fight,
   Our quiet trouble never.

from FUIMUS TROES

Robert Herrick
1591–1674

THE HAG

THE Hag is astride,
   This night for to ride;
The Devil and she together:
   Through thick, and through thin,
   Now out, and then in,
Though ne'r so foul be the weather.

[1] A morris dance

A Thorn or a Burr
She takes for a Spur:
With a lash of a Bramble she rides now,
 Through Brakes and through Briars,
 O'er Ditches and Mires,
She follows the Spirit that guides now.

No Beast, for his food,
Dares now range the wood;
But husht in his lair he lies lurking:
 While mischiefs, by these,
 On Land and on Seas,
At noon of Night are a-working.

The storm will arise,
And trouble the skies;
This night, and more for the wonder,
 The ghost from the Tomb
 Affrighted shall come,
Call'd out by the clap of the Thunder.

THE OLD WIVES' PRAYER

HOLY-ROOD come forth and shield
 Us i' th' Citie, and the Field:
Safely guard us, now and aye,
From the blast that burns by day;
And those sounds that us affright
In the dead of dampish night.
Drive all hurtful Fiends us fro,
By the Time the Cocks first crow.

From *CONNUBII FLORES,*
OR THE WELL-WISHES AT WEDDINGS

CHORUS SACERDOTUM

FROM the Temple to your home
May a thousand blessings come!
And a sweet concurring stream
Of all joys, to join with them.

CHORUS JUVENUM

Happy day
Make no long stay
Here
In thy Sphere;
But give thy place to-night,
That she,
As Thee,
May be
Partaker of this sight.

* * *

CHORUS PASTORUM

Here we present a fleece
To make a piece
Of cloth;
Nor, Fair, must you be loth
Your Finger to apply
To huswiferie.
Then, then begin
To spin:
And (Sweetling) mark you, what a Web will come
Into your Chests, drawn by your painful Thumb.

95

CHORUS MATRONUM

Set you to your Wheel, and wax
　　Rich, by the Ductile Wool and Flax.
Yarn is an Income; and the Huswives thread
The Larder fills with meat; the Bin with bread.

CHORUS SENUM

Let wealth come in by comely thrift,
　　And not by any sordid shift:
　　　　　'Tis haste
　　　　　Makes waste;
　　　　　Extremes have still their fault;
The softest Fire makes the sweetest Mault.
Who gripes too hard the dry and slip'ry sand,
Holds none at all, or little in his hand.

CHORUS VIRGINUM

Goddess of Pleasure, Youth and Peace,
　　Give them the blessing of increase:
And thou *Lucina*, that do'st hear
The vows of those, that children bear;
Whenas her April hour draws near,
Be thou then propitious there.

CHORUS JUVENUM

Far hence be all speech, that may anger move:
Sweet words must nourish soft and gentle Love.

CHORUS OMNIUM

Live in the Love of Doves, and having told
The Ravens' years, go hence more Ripe than old.
96

THE WASSAILE

GIVE way, give way ye Gates, and win
    An easy blessing to your Bin,
And Basket, by our ent'ring in.

May both with manchet stand replete;
Your Larders too so hung with meat,
That though a thousand, thousand eat;

Yet, ere twelve *Moons* shall whirl about
Their silv'ry Spheres, there's none may doubt,
But more's sent in, than was serv'd out.

Next, may your Dairies Prosper so,
As that your Pans no Ebb may know;
But if they do, the more to flow,

Like to a solemn sober Stream
Bankt all with Lilies and the Cream
Of sweetest *Cow-slips* filling Them.

Then, may your Plants be prest with Fruit,
Nor Bee, or Hive you have be mute;
But sweetly sounding like a Lute.

Next may your Duck and teeming Hen
Both to the Cocks-tread, say *Amen;*
And for their two eggs render ten.

Last, may your Harrows, Shares and Ploughs,
Your Stacks, your Stocks, your sweetest Mows,
All prosper by our Virgin-vows.

G

Alas! we bless, but see none here,
That brings us either Ale or Beer;
In a dry-house all things are near.

Let's leave a longer Time to wait,
Where Rust and Cobwebs bind the gate;
And all live here with *needy Fate*.

Where chimneys do for ever weep,
For want of warmth, and stomachs keep
With noise, the servant's eyes from sleep.

It is in vain to sing, or stay
Our free-feet here; but we'l away:
Yet to the Lares this we'l say.

The time will come, when you'l be sad
And reckon this for fortune bad,
T'ave lost the good ye might have had.

CEREMONIES FOR CANDLEMASSE EVE

DOWN with the Rosemary and Bays,
   Down with the Mistletoe;
Instead of Holly, now up-raise
   The greener Box (for show).

The Holly hitherto did sway;
   Let Box now domineer;
Until the dancing Easter-day,
   Or Easter's Eve appear.

Then youthful Box which now hath grace,
    Your houses to renew;
Grown old, surrender must his place,
    Unto the crispèd Yew.

When Yew is out, then Birch comes in,
    And many Flowers beside;
Both of a fresh and fragrant kin
    To honour Whitsuntide.

Green Rushes then, and sweetest Bents,
    With cooler Oaken boughs;
Come in for comely ornaments,
    To re-adorn the house.
Thus times do shift; each thing his turn do's hold;
New things succeed, as former things grow old.

THE DIRGE OF JEPHTHAH'S DAUGHTER: SUNG BY THE VIRGINS

O THOU, the wonder of all days!
    O Paragon, and Pearl of praise!
O Virgin-martyr, ever blest
             Above the rest
Of all the Maiden-Train! We come,
And bring fresh strewings to thy Tomb.

Thus, thus, and thus we compass round
Thy harmless and unhaunted Ground;
And as we sing thy Dirge, we will
             The Daffodil,
And other flowers, lay upon
(The Altar of our love) thy Stone.

Thou wonder of all Maids, li'st here,
Of Daughters all, the Dearest Dear;
The eye of Virgins; nay, the Queen,
                    Of this smooth Green,
And all sweet Meads; from whence we get
The Primrose, and the Violet.

Too soon, too dear did *Jephthah* buy,
By thy sad loss, our liberty:
His was the Bond and Cov'nant, yet
                    Thou paid'st the debt:
Lamented Maid! he won the day,
But for the conquest thou didst pay.

Thy Father brought with him along
The Olive branch, and Victor's Song:
He slew the Ammonites, we know,
                    But to thy woe;
And in the purchase of our Peace,
The Cure was worse than the Disease.

For which obedient zeal of thine,
We offer here, before thy Shrine,
Our sighs for Storax, tears for Wine;
                    And to make fine,
And fresh thy Hearse-cloth, we will, here,
Four times bestrew thee ev'ry year.

Receive, for this thy praise, our tears:
Receive this offering of our Hairs:
Receive these Crystal Vials fill'd
                    With tears, distill'd
From teeming eyes; to these we bring,
Each Maid, her silver Filleting.

To guild thy Tomb; besides, these Cauls,
These Laces, Ribbands, and these Faules,
These Veils, wherewith we use to hide
            The Bashful Bride,
When we conduct her to her Groom:
And, all we lay upon thy Tomb.

No more, no more, since thou art dead,
Shall we ere bring coy Brides to bed;
No more, at yearly Festivals
            We Cowslip balls,
Or chains of Columbines shall make,
For this, or that occasions' sake.

No, no; our Maiden-pleasures be
Wrapt in the winding-sheet, with thee:
'Tis we are dead, though not i' th' grave:
            Or, if we have
One seed of life left, 'tis to keep
A Lent for thee, to fast and weep.

Sleep in thy peace, thy bed of Spice;
And make this place all Paradise:
May Sweets grow here! and smoke from hence,
            Fat Frankincense:
Let Balm and Cassia send their scent
From out thy Maiden-Monument.

May no Wolf howl, or Screech-Owl stir
A wing about thy Sepulchre!
No boisterous winds, or storms, come hither,
            To starve, or wither
Thy soft sweet Earth! but (like a spring)
Love keep it ever flourishing.

May all shy Maids, at wontèd hours,
Come forth, to strew thy Tomb with flow'rs:
May Virgins, when they come to mourn,
                    Male-Incense burn
Upon thine Altar! then return,
And leave thee sleeping in thy Urn.

A CHRISTMAS CAROL

Chor. WHAT sweeter music can we bring
              Than a Carol, for to sing
The birth of this our heavenly King?
Awake the Voice! awake the String!
Heart, Ear, and Eye, and every thing
Awake! the while the active Finger
Runs division with the Singer.

From the Flourish they came to the Song.

1. Dark and dull night, flye hence away,
   And give the honour to this Day,
   That sees *December* turn'd to *May*.

2. If we may ask the reason, say;
   The why, and wherefore all things here
   Seem like the Spring-time of the year?

3. Why do's the chilling Winter's morn
   Smile, like a field beset with corn?
   Or smell, like to a Mead new-shorn,
   Thus, on the sudden? 4. Come and see
   The cause, why things thus fragrant be;
   'Tis He is borne, whose quickning Birth

Gives life and luster, public mirth,
To Heaven, and the under-Earth.

Chor. We see Him come, and know him ours,
Who, with His Sun-shine, and His showers,
Turns all the patient ground to flowers.

1. The Darling of the world is come,
And fit it is, we find a room
To welcome Him. 2. The nobler part
Of all the house here, is the heart,

Chor. Which we will give Him; and bequeath
This Holly, and this Ivy Wreath,
To do Him honour; who's our King,
And Lord of all this Revelling.

John Milton

1608–1674

SONG ON MAY MORNING

NOW the bright morning-star, Day's harbinger,
Comes dancing from the east, and leads with her
The flowery May, who from her green lap throws
The yellow cowslip and the pale primrose.
Hail, bounteous May, that dost inspire
Mirth, and youth, and warm desire!
Woods and groves are of thy dressing;
Hill and dale doth boast thy blessing.
Thus we salute thee with our early song,
And welcome thee, and wish thee long.

SONG OF THE HIERARCHIES ON THE
SEVENTH DAY OF CREATION

GREAT are thy works, Jehovah! infinite
Thy power! what thought can measure thee, or
tongue
Relate thee—greater now in thy return
Than from the Giant-angels? Thee that day
Thy thunders magnified; but to create
Is greater than created to destroy.
Who can impair thee, mighty King, or bound
Thy empire? Easily the proud attempt
Of Spirits apostate, and their counsels vain,
Thou hast repelled, while impiously they thought
Thee to diminish, and from thee withdraw
The number of thy worshippers. Who seeks
To lessen thee, against his purpose, serves
To manifest the more thy might; his evil
Thou usest, and from thence creat'st more good.
Witness this new-made World, another Heaven
From Heaven-gate, not far, founded in view
On the clear hyaline, the glassy sea;
Of amplitude almost immense, with stars
Numerous, and every star perhaps a world
Of destined habitation—but thou know'st
Their seasons; among these the seat of men,
Earth, with her nether ocean circumfused,
Their pleasant dwelling-place. Thrice happy men,
And sons of men, whom God hath thus advanced,
Created in his image, there to dwell
And worship him, and in reward to rule
Over his works, on earth, in sea, or air,

And multiply a race of worshippers
Holy and just! thrice happy, if they know
Their happiness, and persevere upright!

from PARADISE LOST, BOOK VII

ANTHEM OF THE ANGELIC QUIRES AFTER THE LAST TEMPTATION IN THE WILDERNESS

TRUE Image of the Father, whether throned
In the bosom of bliss, and light of light
Conceiving, or, remote from Heaven, enshrined
In fleshly tabernacle and human form,
Wandering the wilderness—whatever place,
Habit, or state, or motion, still expressing
The Son of God, with Godlike force endued
Against the attempter of thy Father's throne
And thief of Paradise! Him long of old
Thou didst debel, and down from Heaven cast
With all his army; now thou hast avenged
Supplanted Adam, and, by vanquishing
Temptation, hast regained lost Paradise,
And frustrated the conquest fraudulent.
He never more henceforth will dare set foot
In Paradise to tempt; his snares are broke.
For, though that seat of earthly bliss be failed
A fairer Paradise is founded now
For Adam and his chosen sons, whom thou,
A Saviour, art come down to reinstall;
Where they shall dwell secure, when time shall be,
Of tempter and temptation without fear.
But thou, Infernal Serpent! shalt not long
Rule in the clouds. Like an autumnal star,
Or lightning, thou shalt fall from Heaven, trod down
Under his feet. For proof, ere this thou feel'st

Thy wound (yet not thy last and deadliest wound)
By this repulse received, and hold'st in Hell
No triumph; in all her gates Abaddon rues
Thy bold attempt. Hereafter learn with awe
To dread the Son of God. He, all unarmed,
Shall chase thee, with the terror of his voice,
From thy demoniac holds, possession foul—
Thee and thy legions; yelling they shall fly,
And beg to hide them in a herd of swine,
Lest he command them down into the Deep,
Bound, and to torment sent before their time.
Hail, Son of the Most High, heir of both Worlds,
Queller of Satan! On thy glorious work
Now enter, and begin to save Mankind.

from PARADISE REGAINED, BOOK IV

Choruses from *SAMSON AGONISTES*

I

O, HOW comely it is, and how reviving
    To the spirits of just men long oppressed,
When God into the hands of their deliverer
Puts invincible might,
To quell the mighty of the earth, the oppressor,
The brute and boisterous force of violent men,
Hardy and industrious to support
Tyrannic power, but raging to pursue
The righteous, and all such as honour truth!
He all their ammunition
And feats of war defeats,
With plain heroic magnitude of mind
And celestial vigour armed;
Their armouries and magazines contemns,
Renders them useless, while
With winged expedition

Swift as the lightning glance he executes
His errand on the wicked, who, surprised,
Lose their defence, distracted and amazed.
　But patience is more oft the exercise
Of saints, the trial of their fortitude,
Making them each his own deliverer,
And victor over all
That tyranny or fortune can inflict,
Either of these is in thy lot,
Samson, with might endued
Above the sons of men; but sight bereaved
May chance to number thee with those
Whom patience finally must crown.

II

　All is best, though we oft doubt
What the unsearchable dispose
Of Highest Wisdom brings about,
And ever best found in the close.
Oft He seems to hide his face,
But unexpectedly returns,
And to his faithful champion hath in place
Bore witness gloriously; whence Gaza mourns,
And all that band them to resist
His uncontrollable intent.
His servants He, with new acquist
Of true experience from this great event,
With peace and consolation hath dismissed,
And calm of mind, all passion spent.

Richard Crashaw
1608–1666

From *IN THE HOLY NATIVITY OF OUR LORD GOD*

(A Hymn as Sung by the Shepherds)

Chorus

COME, we shepherds, whose blest sight
  Hath met Love's noon in Nature's night;
Come, lift we up our loftier song,
And wake the sun that lies too long.

*   *   *   *   *   *

Tell him, Tityrus, where th' hast been,
Tell him, Thyrsis, what th' hast seen.

Tityrus

Gloomy night embraced the place
Where the noble Infant lay.
    The Babe looked up and showed His face;
In spite of darkness, it was day.
    It was Thy day, Sweet! and did rise,
Not from the East, but from Thine eyes.

    Chorus. It was Thy day, etc.

Thyrsis

Winter chid aloud, and sent
The angry North to wage his wars.
    The North forgot his fierce intent,
And left perfumes instead of scars.
    By those sweet eyes' persuasive powers,
Where he meant frost, he scattered flowers.

    Chorus. By those sweet . . .

Both

We saw Thee in Thy balmy-nest,
Young dawn of our eternal Day!
   We saw Thine eyes break from their East,
And chase the trembling shades away.
   We saw Thee; and we blest the sight,
We saw Thee by Thine Own sweet light.

Tityrus

Poor world, (said I), what wilt thou do
To entertain this Starry stranger?
   Is this the best thou canst bestow?
A cold, and not too cleanly, manger?
   Contend, the powers of Heaven and Earth,
To fit a bed for this huge birth?
   Chorus.   Contend, the powers . . .

Thyrsis

Proud world (said I), cease your contest,
And let the mighty Babe alone.
   The phœnix builds the phœnix' nest,
Love's architecture is his own.
   The Babe whose birth embraves this morn
Made His Own bed ere He was born.
   Chorus.   The Babe whose birth . . .

Tityrus

I saw the curled drops, soft and slow,
Come hovering o'er the place's head;
   Offering their whitest sheets of snow
To furnish the fair Infant's bed:
   Forbear, said I; be not too bold,
Your fleece is white, but. 'tis too cold.
   Chorus.   Forbear, said I . . .

Thyrsis

I saw the obsequious Seraphim
Their rosy fleece of fire bestow,
   For well they now can spare their wing,
Since Heaven itself lies here below.
   Well done, said I; but are you sure
Your down so warm will pass for pure?
     Chorus.   Well done, said I . . .

Tityrus

No, no, your King's not yet to seek
Where to repose His royal head;
   See, see, how soon His new-bloom'd cheek
'Twixt mother's breasts is gone to bed.
   Sweet choice, said we! no way but so
Not to lie cold, yet sleep in snow.
     Chorus.   Sweet choice, said we . . .

Both

We saw Thee in Thy balmy nest,
Bright dawn of our eternal Day!
   We saw Thine eyes break from Their East,
And chase the trembling shades away.
   We saw Thee: and we blest the sight,
We saw Thee by Thine Own sweet light.
     Chorus.   We saw Thee . . .

Full Chorus

Welcome, all wonders in one sight!
Eternity shut in a span!
   Summer in Winter, Day in Night!
Heaven in Earth, and God in man!
   Great little One! whose all-embracing birth
Lifts Earth to Heaven, stoops Heaven to Earth.

Andrew Marvell

1621–1678

UPON APPLETON HOUSE (THE GARDEN)

SEE how the flowers, as at parade,
　Under their colours stand displayed:
Each regiment in order grows,
That of the tulip, pink, and rose.
　But when the vigilant patrol
Of stars walks round about the pole,
Their leaves, that to the stalks are curled,
Seem to their staves the ensigns furled.
Then in some flower's belovèd hut,
Each bee, as sentinel, is shut,
And sleeps so too: but if once stirred
She runs you through, nor asks the word.
　Oh, thou, that dear and happy isle,
The garden of the world erewhile,
Thou Paradise of the four seas,
Which Heaven planted us to please,
But, to exclude the world, did guard
With watery, if not flaming sword;
What luckless apple did we taste,
To make us mortal, and thee waste!
　Unhappy! shall we never more
That sweet militia restore,
When gardens only had their towers,
And all the garrisons were flowers;
When roses only arms might bear,
And men did rosy garlands wear?

A DROP OF DEW

SEE, how, the orient dew,
    Shed from the bosom of the Morn,
  Into the blowing roses,
(Yet careless of its mansion new,
For the clear region where 'twas born,)
  Round in itself incloses
And, in its little globe's extent,
Frames, as it can, its native element.
  How it the purple flower does slight,
    Scarce touching where it lies;
  But gazing back upon the skies,
    Shines with a mournful light,
      Like its own tear,
Because so long divided from the sphere.
  Restless it rolls, and unsecure,
    Trembling, lest it grow impure;
  Till the warm Sun pities its pain,
And to the skies exhales it back again.
    So the Soul, that drop, that ray,
Of the clear fountain of Eternal Day,
Could it within the human flower be seen,
  Remembering still its former height,
  Shuns the sweet leaves and blossoms green,
  And, recollecting its own light,
Does, in its pure and circling thoughts express
The greater Heaven in a Heaven less.
    In how coy a figure wound,
    Every way it turns away,
    So the world excluding round,
    Yet receiving in the day,
    Dark beneath, but bright above,
    Here disdaining, there in love.

How loose and easy hence to go;
How girt and ready to ascend;
Moving but on a point below,
It all about does upward bend.
Such did the Manna's sacred dew distil,
White and entire although congealed and chill;
Congealed on earth; but does, dissolving, run
Into the glories of the Almighty Sun.

Thomas Traherne

1637–1674

THANKSGIVINGS FOR THE BEAUTY OF GOD'S PROVIDENCE

I

THESE sweeter far than Lilies are,
No Roses may with these compare!
How these excel
No Tongue can tell!
Which he that well and truly knows,
With praise and joy he goes.
How great and happy's he, that knows his Ways,
To be divine and heavenly Joys!
To whom each City is more brave,
Than Walls of Pearl, or Streets which Gold doth pave:
Whose open eyes
Behold the Skies;
Who loves their Wealth and Beauty more,
Than Kings love golden Ore!

Who sees the heavenly antient Ways,
Of GOD the Lord, with Joy and Praise;
 More than the Skies,
 With open Eyes,
Doth prize them all: yea more than Gems
 And Regal Diadems.
That more esteemeth Mountains as they are,
Than if they Gold and Silver were:
To whom the *SUN* more pleasure brings,
Than Crowns and Thrones, and Palaces, to Kings.
 That knows his Ways,
 To be the Joys,
And Way of God. These things who knows,
 With Joy and Praise he goes.

from SERIOUS AND PATHETICAL CONTEMPLATION
OF THE MERCIES OF GOD

Jeremy Taylor
1613–1667

A HYMN FOR CHRISTMAS DAY

AWAKE, my soul, and come away.
 Put on thy best array;
Lest if thou longer stay
Thou lose some minutes of so blest a day.
     Go run
And bid good-morrow to the sun;
Welcome his safe return
      To Capricorn.
 And to that great morn
 Wherein a God was born,
 Whose story none can tell
But He whose every word's a miracle.

To-day Almightiness grew weak.
The Word itself was mute and could not speak.
That Jacob's star which made the sun
To dazzle if he durst look on,
Now mantled o'er in Bethlehem's night,
Borrowed a star to show him light.
He that begirt each zone,
To whom both poles are one,
Who grasped the Zodiac in His hand
And made it move or stand,
Is now by nature man,
By stature but a span;
Eternity is now grown short;
A king is born without a court;
The water thirsts; the fountain's dry;
And life, being born, made apt to die.

Chorus

 Then let our praises emulate and vie
  With His humility!
 Since He's exiled from the skies
  That we might rise—
 From low estate of men
 Let's sing Him up again!
 Each man wind up his heart
 To bear a part
 In that angelic choir and show
 His glory high as He was low.
 Let's sing towards men goodwill and charity,
  Peace upon earth, glory to God on High!
   Hallelujah! Hallelujah!

from FESTIVAL HYMNS

Henry Vaughan
1621–1695

THE REVIVAL

UNFOLD! unfold! Take in His light,
　　Who makes thy cares more short than night.
The joys which with His day-star rise
He deals to all but drowsy eyes;
And, what the men of this world miss,
Some drops and dews of future bliss.

Hark! how the winds have changed their note,
And with warm whispers call thee out!
The frosts are past, the storms are gone,
And backward life at last comes on;
The lofty groves in express joys
Reply unto the turtle's voice,
And here in dust and dirt, O here,
The lilies of His love appear!

SUN-DAYS

BRIGHT shadows of true rest! some shoots of bliss,
　　Heaven once a week;
The next world's gladness prepossessed in this;
　　A day to seek
Eternity in time; the steps by which
　We climb above all ages; lamps that light
Man through his heap of dark days: and the rich
　And full redemption of the whole week's flight.

The pulleys unto headlong man; Time's bower;
    The narrow way;
Transplanted Paradise; God's walking hour,
    The cool o' th' day!
The creature's jubilee; God's parle with dust;
Heaven here; man on those hills of myrrh and flowers;
Angels descending; the returns of trust;
A gleam of glory after six days' showers.

The Church's love-feasts; Time's prerogative
    And interest
Deducted from the whole; the combs, and hive,
    And home of rest.
The milky way chalked out with suns; a clue
That guides through erring hours; and in full story
A taste of heaven on earth; the pledge and cue
Of a full feast; and the out-courts of glory.

John Hall of Durham
1627–1656

A PASTORAL HYMN

HAPPY choristers of air,
    Who by your nimble flight draw near
His throne, Whose wondrous story,
    And unconfinèd glory
Your notes still carol, whom your sound,
And whom your plumy pipes rebound.

Yet do the lazy snails no less
The greatness of our Lord confess,
    And those whom weight hath chained,
    And to the earth restrained,
Their ruder voices do as well,
Yes, and the speechless fishes tell.

Great Lord, from whom each tree receives,
Then pays again, as rent, his leaves;
  Thou dost in purple set
  The rose and violet,
And giv'st the sickly lily white;
Yet in them all Thy name dost write.

John Dryden
1631–1700

A SONG FOR ST CECILIA'S DAY

FROM harmony, from heavenly harmony,
  This universal frame began:
When nature underneath a heap
  Of jarring atoms lay,
  And could not heave her head,
The tuneful voice was heard from high,
  "Arise, ye more than dead!"
Then cold, and hot, and moist, and dry,
  In order to their stations leap,
  And Music's power obey.
From harmony, from heavenly harmony,
  This universal frame began:
  From harmony to harmony
Through all the compass of the notes it ran,
The diapason closing full in Man.

What passion cannot Music raise and quell?
  When Jubal struck the chorded shell,
  His listening brethren stood around,
    And, wondering, on their faces fell
  To worship that celestial sound:

Less than a God they thought there could not dwell
    Within the hollow of that shell,
    That spoke so sweetly, and so well.
What passion cannot Music raise and quell?

    The trumpet's loud clangour
      Excites us to arms,
    With shrill notes of anger,
      And mortal alarms.
    The double double double beat
      Of the thundering drum
      Cries Hark! the foes come;
Charge, charge, 'tis too late to retreat!

    The soft complaining flute,
    In dying notes, discovers
    The woes of hopeless lovers,
Whose dirge is whisper'd by the warbling lute.

    Sharp violins proclaim
    Their jealous pangs and desperation,
    Fury, frantic indignation,
    Depth of pains, and height of passion,
      For the fair, disdainful dame.

    But O, what art can teach,
    What human voice can reach,
      The sacred organ's praise?
    Notes inspiring holy love,
    Notes that wing their heavenly ways
      To mend the choirs above.

Orpheus could lead the savage race;
And trees unrooted left their place,
    Sequacious of the lyre;

But bright Cecilia rais'd the wonder higher:
When to her organ vocal breath was given,
   An angel heard, and straight appear'd
    Mistaking Earth for Heaven.

GRAND CHORUS

As from the power of sacred lays
   The spheres began to move,
And sung the great Creator's praise
   To all the Blest above;
So when the last and dreadful hour
This crumbling pageant shall devour,
The trumpet shall be heard on high,
The dead shall live, the living die,
And Music shall untune the sky!

Joseph Addison

1672–1719

ODE

THE Spacious Firmament on high,
   With all the blue Ethereal Sky,
And spangled Heav'ns, a Shining Frame,
Their great Original proclaim:
Th' unwearied Sun, from Day to Day
Does his Creator's Power display,
And publishes to every Land
The Work of an Almighty Hand.

Soon as the Evening Shades prevail,
The Moon takes up the wondrous Tale,
And nightly to the list'ning Earth
Repeats the Story of her Birth:

Whilst all the Stars that round her burn,
And all the Planets, in their turn,
Confirm the Tidings as they roll,
And spread the Truth from Pole to Pole.

What though, in solemn Silence, all
Move round the dark terrestrial Ball?
What tho' nor real Voice nor Sound
Amid their radiant Orbs be found?
In Reason's Ear they all rejoice,
And utter forth a glorious Voice,
For ever singing, as they shine,
"The Hand that made us is Divine."

published in The Spectator (1712)

Henry Fielding
1707–1754
HUNTING SONG

THE dusky Night rides down the Sky,
  And ushers in the Morn;
The Hounds all join in glorious Cry,
  The Huntsman winds his Horn:
  And a Hunting we will go.

The Wife around her Husband throws
  Her Arms, and begs his Stay;
"My Dear, it rains, and hails, and snows,
  You will not hunt to-day."
  But a Hunting we will go.

"A brushing Fox in yonder Wood,
  Secure to find we seek;
For why, I carried sound and good
  A Cartload there last Week.
  And a Hunting we will go.

Away he goes, he flies the Rout,
  Their Steeds all spur and switch;
Some are thrown in, and some thrown out,
  And some thrown in the Ditch:
    But a Hunting we will go.

At length his Strength to Faintness worn,
  Poor *Reynard* ceases Flight;
Then, hungry, homeward we return,
  To feast away the Night:
    Then a Drinking we will go.

from DON QUIXOTE IN ENGLAND

William Collins

1721–1759

ODE TO EVENING

IF aught of oaten stop, or pastoral song,
  May hope, chaste Eve, to soothe thy modest ear,
    Like thy own solemn springs,
    Thy springs and dying gales;

O nymph reserved, while now the bright-haired sun
Sits in yon western tent, whose cloudy skirts,
    With brede ethereal wove,
    O'erhang his wavy bed:

Now air is hush'd, save where the weak-eyed bat
With short shrill shriek flits by on leathern wing,
    Or where the beetle winds
    His small but sullen horn,

As oft he rises, 'midst the twilight path
Against the pilgrim borne in heedless hum;
    Now teach me, maid composed,
    To breathe some soften'd strain,

122

Whose numbers, stealing through thy darkening vale,
May not unseemly with its stillness suit,
    As, musing slow, I hail
    Thy genial loved return!

For when thy folding-star arising shows
His paly circlet, at his warning lamp
    The fragrant hours, and elves
    Who slept in buds the day,

And many a nymph who wreathes her brows with sedge,
And sheds the freshening dew, and, lovelier still,
    The pensive pleasures sweet,
    Prepare thy shadowy car:

Then lead, calm votaress, where some sheety lake
Cheers the lone heath, or some time-hallowed pile,
    Or upland fallows grey
    Reflect its last cool gleam.

Or if chill blustering winds, or driving rain,
Prevent my willing feet, be mine the hut
    That from the mountain's side
    Views wilds and swelling floods,

And hamlets brown, and dim-discover'd spires,
And hears their simple bell, and marks o'er all
    Thy dewy fingers draw
    The gradual dusky veil.

While Spring shall pour his show'rs, as oft he wont,
And bathe thy breathing tresses, meekest Eve!
    While Summer loves to sport
    Beneath thy lingering light;

While sallow Autumn fills thy lap with leaves,
Or Winter, yelling through the troublous air,
    Affrights thy shrinking train,
    And rudely rends thy robes:

So long, regardful of thy quiet rule,
Shall Fancy, Friendship, Science, rose-lipp'd Health
    Thy gentlest influence own,
    And hymn thy favourite name!

Christopher Smart
1722–1771

From *A SONG TO DAVID*

. . . SWEET is the dew that falls betimes,
    And drops upon the leafy limes;
    Sweet Hermon's fragrant air:
Sweet is the lily's silver bell,
And sweet the wakeful tapers smell,
    That watch for early pray'r.

Sweet the young nurse with love intense,
Which smiles o'er sleeping innocence;
    Sweet when the lost arrive:
Sweet the musician's ardour beats,
While his vague mind's in quest of sweets,
    The choicest flow'rs to hive.

Sweeter in all the strains of love,
The language of thy turtle dove,
    Pair'd to thy swelling chord;
Sweeter with ev'ry grace endu'd,
The glory of thy gratitude,
    Respir'd unto the Lord.

Strong is the horse upon his speed;
Strong in pursuit the rapid glede,
    Which makes at once his game;
Strong the tall ostrich on the ground;
Strong through the turbulent profound
    Shoots xiphias to his aim.

Strong is the lion—like a coal
His eyeball—like a bastion's mole
    His chest against the foes:
Strong the gier-eagle on his sail,
Strong against tide, th'enormous whale
    Emerges, as he goes.

But stronger still, in earth and air,
And in the sea, the man of pray'r;
    And far beneath the tide;
And in the seat to faith assign'd,
Where ask is have, where seek is find,
    Where knock is open wide.

Beauteous the fleet before the gale;
Beauteous the multitudes in mail,
    Rank'd arms and crested heads:
Beauteous the garden's umbrage mild,
Walk, water, meditated wild,
    And all the bloomy beds.

Beauteous the moon full on the lawn;
And beauteous, when the veil's withdrawn,
    The virgin to her spouse:
Beauteous the temple deck'd and fill'd,
When to the heav'n of heav'ns they build
    Their heart-directed vows.

Beauteous, yea beauteous more than these,
The shepherd king upon his knees,
    For his momentous trust;
With wish of infinite conceit,
For man, beast, mute, the small and great,
    And prostrate dust to dust.

Precious the bounteous widow's mite;
And precious, for extreme delight,
    The largess from the churl:
Precious the ruby's blushing blaze,
And alba's blest imperial rays,
    And pure cerulean pearl.

Precious the penitential tear;
And precious is the sigh sincere,
    Acceptable to God:
And precious are the winning flow'rs,
In gladsome Israel's feast of bow'rs,
    Bound on the hallow'd sod.

More precious that diviner part
Of David, ev'n the Lord's own heart,
    Great, beautiful, and new:
In all things where it was intent,
In all extremes, in each event,
    Proof—answ'ring true to true.

Glorious the sun in mid career;
Glorious th' assembled fires appear;
    Glorious the comet's train:
Glorious the trumpet and alarm;
Glorious th' almighty stretch'd-out arm;
    Glorious th' enraptur'd main:

Glorious the northern lights astream;
Glorious the song, when God's the theme;
　　Glorious the thunder's roar:
Glorious hosanna from the den;
Glorious the catholic amen;
　　Glorious the martyr's gore:

Glorious—more glorious is the crown
Of Him, that brought salvation down
　　By meekness, call'd thy Son;
Thou at stupendous truth believ'd,
And now the matchless deed's achiev'd,
　　DETERMIN'D, DAR'D, and DONE.

William Blake

1757–1827

TO SPRING

O THOU with dewy locks, who lookest down
　　Thro' the clear windows of the morning, turn
Thine angel eyes upon our western isle,
Which in full choir hails thy approach, O Spring!

The hills tell each other, and the list'ning
Valleys hear; all our longing eyes are turnèd
Up to thy bright pavilions: issue forth,
And let thy holy feet visit our clime.

Come o'er the eastern hills, and let our winds
Kiss thy perfumèd garments; let us taste
Thy morn and evening breath; scatter thy pearls
Upon our love-sick land that mourns for thee.

127

O deck her forth with thy fair fingers; pour
Thy soft kisses on her bosom; and put
Thy golden crown upon her languish'd head,
Whose modest tresses were bound up for thee.

TO SUMMER

O THOU who passest thro' our valleys in
Thy strength, curb thy fierce steeds, allay the heat
That flames from their large nostrils! thou, O Summer,
Oft pitched'st here thy golden tent, and oft
Beneath our oaks hast slept, while we beheld
With joy thy ruddy limbs and flourishing hair.

Beneath our thickest shades we oft have heard
Thy voice, when noon upon his fervid car
Rode o'er the deep of heaven; beside our springs
Sit down, and in our mossy valleys, on
Some bank beside a river clear, throw thy
Silk draperies off, and rush into the stream;
Our valleys love the Summer in his pride.

Our bards are fam'd who strike the silver wire:
Our youth are bolder than the southern swains:
Our maidens fairer in the sprightly dance:
We lack not songs, nor instruments of joy,
Nor echoes sweet, nor waters clear as heaven,
Nor laurel wreaths against the sultry heat.

TO AUTUMN

O AUTUMN, laden with fruit, and stainèd
With the blood of the grape, pass not, but sit
Beneath my shady roof; there thou may'st rest,
And tune thy jolly voice to my fresh pipe,

And all the daughters of the year shall dance!
Sing now the lusty songs of fruits and flowers.

"The narrow bud opens her beauties to
The sun, and love runs in her thrilling veins;
Blossoms hang round the brows of Morning, and
Flourish down the bright cheek of modest Eve,
Till clust'ring Summer breaks forth into singing,
And feather'd clouds strew flowers round her head.

"The spirits of the air live on the smells
Of fruit; and Joy, with pinions light, roves round
The gardens, or sits singing in the trees."
Thus sang the jolly Autumn as he sat;
Then rose, girded himself, and o'er the bleak
Hills fled from our sight; but left his golden load.

TO WINTER

"O WINTER! bar thine adamantine doors:
The north is thine; there hast thou built thy dark
Deep-founded habitation. Shake not thy roofs,
Nor bend thy pillars with thine iron car."

He hears me not, but o'er the yawning deep
Rides heavy; his storms are unchain'd, sheathèd
In ribbèd steel; I dare not lift mine eyes,
For he hath rear'd his sceptre o'er the world.

Lo! now the direful monster, whose skin clings
To his strong bones, strides o'er the groaning rocks:
He withers all in silence, and in his hand
Unclothes the earth, and freezes up frail life.

He takes his seat upon the cliffs,—the mariner
Cries in vain. Poor little wretch, that deal'st
With storms!—till heaven smiles, and the monster
Is driv'n yelling to his caves beneath mount Hecla.

TO THE EVENING STAR

THOU fair-hair'd angel of the evening,
  Now, whilst the sun rests on the mountains, light
Thy bright torch of love; thy radiant crown
Put on, and smile upon our evening bed!
Smile on our loves, and while thou drawest the
Blue curtains of the sky, scatter thy silver dew
On every flower that shuts its sweet eyes
In timely sleep. Let thy west wind sleep on
The lake; speak silence with thy glimmering eyes,
And wash the dusk with silver. Soon, full soon,
Dost thou withdraw; then the wolf rages wide,
And the lion glares thro' the dun forest:
The fleeces of our flocks are cover'd with
Thy sacred dew: protect them with thine influence.

TO MORNING

O HOLY virgin! clad in purest white,
  Unlock heav'n's golden gates, and issue forth;
Awake the dawn that sleeps in heaven; let light
Rise from the chambers of the east, and bring
The honey'd dew that cometh on waking day.
O radiant morning, salute the sun
Rous'd like a huntsman to the chase, and with
Thy buskin'd feet appear upon our hills.

From MILTON

AND did those feet in ancient time
  Walk upon England's mountains green?
And was the holy Lamb of God
  On England's pleasant pastures seen?

And did the Countenance Divine
   Shine forth upon our clouded hills?
And was Jerusalem builded here
   Among these dark Satanic Mills?

Bring me my bow of burning gold!
   Bring me my arrows of desire!
Bring me my spear! O clouds, unfold!
   Bring me my chariot of fire!

I will not cease from mental fight,
   Nor shall my sword sleep in my hand,
Till we have built Jerusalem
   In England's green and pleasant land.

From *JERUSALEM*

ENGLAND! awake! awake! awake!
   Jerusalem thy sister calls!
Why wilt thou sleep the sleep of death,
   And close her from thy ancient walls?

Thy hills and valleys felt her feet
   Gently upon their bosoms move:
Thy gates beheld sweet Zion's ways;
   Then was a time of joy and love.

And now the time returns again:
   Our souls exult, and London's towers
Receive the Lamb of God to dwell
   In England's green and pleasant bowers.

A SONG OF LIBERTY

THE Eternal Female groan'd! It was heard over all the Earth.

2. Albion's coast is sick, silent. The American meadows faint!

3. Shadows of prophecy shiver along by the lakes and the rivers, and mutter across the ocean. France, rend down thy dungeon!

4. Golden Spain, burst the barriers of old Rome!

5. Cast thy keys, O Rome! into the deep, down falling, even to eternity down falling,

6. And weep.

7. In her trembling hands she took the new-born terror, howling.

8. On those infinite mountains of light, now barr'd out by the Atlantic sea, the new-born fire stood before the starry king!

9. Flagg'd with grey-brow'd snows and thunderous visages, the jealous wings wav'd over the deep.

10. The speary hand burnèd aloft, unbuckled was the shield; forth went the hand of Jealousy among the flaming hair, and hurl'd the new-born wonder thro' the starry night.

11. The fire, the fire, is falling!

12. Look up! look up! O citizen of London, enlarge thy countenance! O Jew, leave counting gold! return to thy oil and wine. O African! black African! Go, wingèd thought, widen his forehead!

13. The fiery limbs, the flaming hair, shot like the sinking sun into the western sea.

14. Wak'd from his eternal sleep, the hoary element, roaring, fled away.

15. Down rush'd, beating his wings in vain, the jealous King; his grey-brow'd counsellors, thunderous warriors, curl'd veterans, among helms, and shields, and chariots, horses, elephants, banners, castles, slings, and rocks,

16. Falling, rushing, ruining! buried in the ruins, on Urthona's dens;

17. All night beneath the ruins; then, their sullen flames ended, emerge round the gloomy King.

18. With thunder and fire, leading his starry hosts thro' the waste wilderness, he promulgates his ten commands, glancing his beamy eyelids over the deep in dark dismay.

19. Where the son of fire in his eastern cloud, while the morning plumes her golden breast,

20. Spurning the clouds written with curses, stamps the stony law to dust, loosing the eternal horses from the dens of night, crying: *Empire is no more! and now the lion and the wolf shall cease.*

CHORUS

Let the Priests of the Raven of dawn no longer, in deadly black, with hoarse note curse the sons of joy! Nor his accepted brethren—whom, tyrant, he calls free—lay the bound or build the roof! Nor pale religion's lechery call that Virginity that wishes but acts not!

For everything that lives is Holy!

Robert Burns
1759–1796

MACPHERSON'S FAREWELL

FAREWELL, ye dungeons dark and strong,
 The wretch's destinie!
Macpherson's time will not be long
 On yonder gallows-tree.
  Sae rantingly, sae wantonly,
   Sae dauntingly gaed he:
  He played a spring, and danced it round,
   Below the gallows-tree.

Oh! what is death but parting breath?
 On mony a bloody plain
I've dared his face, and in this place
 I scorn him yet again!
  Sae rantingly, etc.

Untie these bands from off my hands,
 And bring to me my sword!
And there's no a man in all Scotland
 But I'll brave him at a word.
  Sàe rantingly, etc.

I've lived a life of sturt and strife;
 I die by treacherie:
It burns my heart I must depart,
 And not avengèd be.
  Sae rantingly, etc.

Now farewell light—thou sunshine bright
 And all beneath the sky!
May coward shame disdain his name,
 The wretch that dares not die!
  Sae rantingly, etc.

Leigh Hunt
1784–1859

TRIO AND CHORUS
OF STOUT HEART, TOIL, EXERCISE AND
REAPERS AND VINE-GATHERERS

ALL joy to the giver of wine and of corn,
  With her elbow at ease on her well-filled horn;
    To the sunny cheek brown,
    And the shady wheat crown,
And the ripe golden locks that come smelling of morn.
Stout Heart. 'Tis she in our veins that puts daily delight;
Toil. 'Tis she in our beds puts us kindly at night;
Exercise. And taps at our doors in the morning bright.
    Chorus. Then joy to the giver, etc.

We'll sling on our flaskets, and forth with the sun,
With our trim-ancled yoke-fellows, every one;
    We'll gather and reap
    With our arm at a sweep,
And oh! for the dancing when all is done;
Exercise. Yes, yes, we'll be up when the singing-bird starts;
Toil. We'll level her harvests, and fill up her carts;
Stout Heart. And shake off fatigue with our bounding
        hearts:
    Chorus. Then hey for the flaskets, etc.

from THE DESCENT OF LIBERTY

Thomas Love Peacock
1785–1866

THE BRILLIANCIES OF WINTER

LAST of flowers, in tufts around
  Shines the gorse's golden bloom:

135

Milk-white lichens clothe the ground
'Mid the flowerless heath and broom:
Bright are holly-berries, seen
Red, through leaves of glossy green.

Brightly, as on the rocks they leap,
Shine the sea-waves, white with spray:
Brightly, in the dingles deep,
Gleams the river's foaming way;
Brightly through the distance show
Mountain-summits clothed in snow.

Brightly, where the torrents bound,
Shines the frozen colonnade,
Which the black rocks, dripping round,
And the flying spray have made:
Bright the ice-drops on the ash
Leaning o'er the cataract's dash.

Bright the hearth, where feast and song
Crown the warrior's hour of peace,
While the snow-storm drives along,
Bidding war's worse tempest cease;
Bright the hearth-flame, flashing clear
On the up-hung shield and spear.

Bright the torchlight of the hall
When the wintry night-winds blow;
Brightest when its splendours fall
On the mead-cup's sparkling flow:
While the maiden's smile of light
Makes the brightness trebly bright.

Close the portals; pile the hearth;
Strike the harp; the feast pursue;

Brim the horns: fire, music, mirth,
Mead and love, are winter's due.
Spring to purple conflict calls
Swords that shine on winter's walls.

from THE MISFORTUNES OF ELPHIN

Percy Bysshe Shelley
1792–1822

AUTUMN: A DIRGE

THE warm sun is failing, the bleak wind is wailing,
  The bare boughs are sighing, the pale flowers are
dying,
          And the Year
On the earth her death-bed, in a shroud of leaves dead,
            Is lying.
          Come, Months, come away,
          From November to May,
          In your saddest array;
          Follow the bier
          Of the dead cold Year,
And like dim shadows watch by her sepulchre.

The chill rain is falling, the nipped worm is crawling,
The rivers are swelling, the thunder is knelling
            For the Year;
The blithe swallows are flown, and the lizards each gone
            To his dwelling;
          Come, Months, come away;
          Put on white, black, and gray;
          Let your light sisters play—
          Ye, follow the bier
          Of the dead cold Year,
And make her grave green with tear on tear.

137

From *PROMETHEUS UNBOUND*

I

CHORUS OF SPIRITS

FROM unremembered ages we
  Gentle guides and guardians be
Of heaven-oppressed mortality;
And we breathe, and sicken not,
The atmosphere of human thought:
Be it dim, and dank, and gray,
Like a storm-extinguished day,
Travelled o'er by dying gleams;
  Be it bright as all between
Cloudless skies and windless streams,
  Silent, liquid, and serene;
As the birds within the wind,
  As the fish within the wave,
As the thoughts of man's own mind
  Float through all above the grave;
We make there our liquid lair,
Voyaging cloudlike and unpent
Through the boundless element:
Thence we bear the prophecy
Which begins and ends in thee!

FIRST SPIRIT

On a battle-trumpet's blast
I fled hither, fast, fast, fast,
'Mid the darkness upward cast.
From the dust of creeds outworn,
From the tyrant's banner torn.
Gathering 'round me, onward borne,
There was mingled many a cry—
Freedom! Hope! Death! Victory!
Till they faded through the sky;

And one sound, above, around,
One sound beneath, around, above,
Was moving; 'twas the soul of Love;
'Twas the hope, the prophecy,
Which begins and ends in thee.

SECOND SPIRIT

A rainbow's arch stood on the sea,
Which rocked beneath, immovably;
And the triumphant storm did flee,
Like a conqueror, swift and proud,
Between, with many a captive cloud,
A shapeless, dark and rapid crowd,
Each by lightning riven in half:
I heard the thunder hoarsely laugh:
Mighty fleets were strewn like chaff
And spread beneath a hell of death
O'er the white waters. I alit
On a great ship lightning-split,
And speeded hither on the sigh
Of one who gave an enemy
His plank, then plunged aside to die.

THIRD SPIRIT

I sate beside a sage's bed,
And the lamp was burning red
Near the book where he had fed,
When a Dream with plumes of flame,
To his pillow hovering came,
And I knew it was the same
Which had kindled long ago
Pity, eloquence, and woe;
And the world awhile below
Wore the shade, its lustre made.

139

It has borne me here as fleet
As Desire's lightning feet:
I must ride it back ere morrow
Or the sage will wake in sorrow.

FOURTH SPIRIT

On a poet's lips I slept
Dreaming like a love-adept
In the sound his breathing kept;
Nor seeks nor finds he mortal blisses,
But feeds on the aëreal kisses
Of shapes that haunt thought's wildernesses.
He will watch from dawn to gloom
The lake-reflected sun illume
The yellow bees in the ivy-bloom,
Nor heed nor see, what things they be;
But from these create he can
Forms more real than living man,
Nurslings of immortality!
One of these awakened me,
And I sped to succour thee.

CHORUS OF SPIRITS

Hast thou beheld the form of Love?

FIFTH SPIRIT

As over wide dominions
I sped, like some swift cloud that wings the wide air's
wildernesses,
That planet-crested shape swept by on lightning-braided
pinions,
Scattering the liquid joy of life from his ambrosial tresses:
His footsteps paved the world with light; but as I passed
'twas fading,

And hollow Ruin yawned behind: great sages bound
   in madness,
And headless patriots, and pale youths who perished,
   unupbraiding,
   Gleamed in the night. I wandered o'er, till thou, O
     King of sadness,
   Turned by thy smile the worst I saw to recollected
     gladness.

SIXTH SPIRIT

Ah, sister! Desolation is a delicate thing:
   It walks not on the earth, it floats not on the air,
But treads with lulling footstep, and fans with silent wing
   The tender hopes which in their hearts the best and
     gentlest bear;
Who, soothed to false repose by the fanning plumes above
   And the music-stirring motion of its soft and busy feet,
Dream visions of aëreal joy, and call the monster, Love,
   And wake, and find the shadow Pain, as he whom now
     we greet.

CHORUS

Though Ruin now Love's shadow be,
Following him, destroyingly,
   On Death's white and wingèd steed,
Which the fleetest cannot flee,
   Trampling down both flower and weed,
Man and beast, and foul and fair,
Like a tempest through the air;
Thou shalt quell this horseman grim,
Woundless though in heart or limb.

Prometheus: Spirits! how know ye this shall be?

141

CHORUS

In the atmosphere we breathe,
As buds grow red when the snow-storms flee,
From Spring gathering up beneath,
Whose mild winds shake the elder brake,
And the wandering herdsmen know
That the white-thorn soon will blow:
Wisdom, Justice, Love, and Peace,
When they struggle to increase,
Are to us as soft winds be
To shepherd boys, the prophecy
Which begins and ends in thee.

II

CHORUS OF ECHOES

Echoes we: listen!
We cannot stay:
As dew-stars glisten
Then fade away—
Child of Ocean!

O, follow, follow,
As our voice recedeth
Through the caverns hollow,
Where the forest spreadeth;

(More distant)
O, follow, follow!
Through the caverns hollow,
As the song floats thou pursue,
Where the wild bee never flew,
Through the noontide darkness deep,
By the odour-breathing sleep
Of faint night flowers, and the waves
At the fountain-lighted caves,

While our music, wild and sweet,
Mocks thy gently falling feet,
   Child of Ocean!

  In the world unknown
  Sleeps a voice unspoken;
  By thy step alone
   Can its rest be broken;
   Child of Ocean!

 O, follow, follow!
 Through the caverns hollow,
As the song floats thou pursue,
By the woodland noontide dew;
By the forest, lakes, and fountains,
Through the many-folded mountains;
To the rents, and gulfs, and chasms,
Where the Earth reposed from spasms,
On the day when He and thou
Parted, to commingle now;
   Child of Ocean!

III

SONG OF SPIRITS

To the deep, to the deep,
     Down, down!
Through the shade of sleep,
Through the cloudy strife
Of Death and of Life;
Through the veil and the bar
Of things which seem and are
Even to the steps of the remotest throne,
     Down, down!

While the sound whirls around,
        Down, down!
As the fawn draws the hound,
As the lightning the vapour,
As a weak moth the taper;
Death, despair; love, sorrow;
Time both; to-day, to-morrow;
As steel obeys the spirit of the stone,
        Down, down!

Through the gray, void abysm,
        Down, down!
Where the air is no prism,
And the moon and stars are not,
And the cavern-crags wear not
The radiance of Heaven,
Nor the gloom to Earth given,
Where there is One pervading, One alone,
        Down, down!

In the depth of the deep,
        Down, down!
Like veiled lightning asleep,
Like the spark nursed in embers,
The last look Love remembers,
Like a diamond, which shines
On the dark wealth of mines,
A spell is treasured but for thee alone.
        Down, down!

We have bound thee, we guide thee;
        Down, down!
With the bright form beside thee;

Resist not the weakness,
Such strength is in meekness
That the Eternal, the Immortal,
Must unloose through life's portal
The snake-like Doom coiled underneath his throne
By that alone.

Last Chorus from *HELLAS*

THE world's great age begins anew,
  The golden years return,
The earth doth like a snake renew
  Her winter weeds outworn:
Heaven smiles, and faiths and empires gleam,
Like wrecks of a dissolving dream.

A brighter Hellas rears its mountains
  From waves serener far;
A new Peneus rolls his fountains
  Against the morning star.
Where fairer Tempes bloom, there sleep
Young Cyclads on a sunnier deep.

A loftier Argo cleaves the main,
  Fraught with a later prize;
Another Orpheus sings again,
  And loves, and weeps, and dies.
A new Ulysses leaves once more
Calypso for his native shore.

Oh, write no more the tale of Troy,
  If earth Death's scroll must be!
Nor mix with Laian rage the joy
  Which dawns upon the free:
Although a subtler Sphinx renew
Riddles of death Thebes never knew.

Another Athens shall arise,
  And to remoter time
Bequeath, like sunset to the skies,
  The splendour of its prime;
And leave, if nought so bright may live,
All earth can take or Heaven can give.

Saturn and Love their long repose
  Shall burst, more bright and good
Than all who fell, than One who rose,
  Than many unsubdued:
Not gold, not blood, their altar dowers,
But votive tears and symbol flowers.

Oh, cease! must hate and death return?
  Cease! must men kill and die?
Cease! drain not to its dregs the urn
  Of bitter prophecy.
The world is weary of the past,
Oh, might it die or rest at last!

John Clare
1793–1864

SONG'S ETERNITY

WHAT is song's eternity?
    Come and see.
Can it noise and bustle be?
    Come and see.
Praises sung or praises said
    Can it be?
Wait awhile and these are dead—
    Sigh, sigh;
Be they high or lowly bred
    They die.

What is song's eternity?
    Come and see.
Melodies of earth and sky,
    Here they be.
Song once sung to Adam's ears
    Can it be?
Ballads of six thousand years
    Thrive, thrive;
Songs awaken with the spheres
    Alive.

Mighty songs that miss decay,
    What are they?
Crowds and cities pass away
    Like a day.
Books are out and books are read;
    What are they?
Years will lay them with the dead—
    Sigh, sigh;
Trifles unto nothing wed,
    They die.

Dreamers, mark the honey bee;
    Mark the tree
Where the blue cap *"tootle tee"*
    Sings a glee
Sung to Adam and to Eve—
    Here they be.
When floods covered every bough,
    Noah's ark
Heard that ballad singing now;
    Hark, hark,

"Tootle, tootle, tootle tee"—
    Can it be

147

Pride and fame must shadows be?
    Come and see—
Every season owns her own;
    Bird and bee
Sing creation's music on;
    Nature's glee
Is in every mood and tone
    Eternity.

John Keats

1795–1821

SONG OF THE SHEPHERDS OF LATMOS

O THOU, whose mighty palace roof doth hang
  From jagged trunks, and overshadoweth
Eternal whispers, glooms, the birth, life, death
Of unseen flowers in heavy peacefulness;
Who lov'st to see the hamadryads dress
Their ruffled locks where meeting hazels darken;
And through whole solemn hours dost sit, and hearken
The dreary melody of bedded reeds—
In desolate places, where dank moisture breeds
The pipy hemlock to strange overgrowth;
Bethinking thee, how melancholy loth
Thou wast to lose fair Syrinx—do thou now,
By thy love's milky brow!
By all the trembling mazes that she ran,
Hear us, great Pan!

   O thou, for whose soul-soothing quiet, turtles
Passion their voices cooingly 'mong myrtles,

What time thou wanderest at eventide
Through sunny meadows, that outskirt the side
Of thine enmossed realms: O thou, to whom
Broad-leaved fig trees even now foredoom
Their ripen'd fruitage; yellow girted bees
Their golden honeycombs; our village leas
Their fairest blossomed beans and poppied corn;
The chuckling linnet its five young unborn,
To sing for thee; low creeping strawberries
Their summer coolness; pent-up butterflies
Their freckled wings; yea, the fresh budding year
All its completions—be quickly near,
By every wind that nods the mountain pine,
O forester divine!

   Thou, to whom every fawn and satyr flies
For willing service; whether to surprise
The squatted hare while in half-sleeping fit;
Or upward ragged precipices flit
To save poor lambkins from the eagle's maw;
Or by mysterious enticement draw
Bewildered shepherds to their path again;
Or to tread breathless round the frothy main,
And gather up all fancifullest shells
For thee to tumble into Naiads' cells,
And, being hidden, laugh at their outpeeping;
Or to delight thee with fantastic leaping,
The while they pelt each other on the crown
With silvery oak apples, and fir cones brown—
By all the echoes that about thee ring,
Hear us, O satyr king!

O Hearkener to the loud-clapping shears,
While ever and anon to his shorn peers
A ram goes bleating: Winder of the horn,
When snouted wild-boars routing tender corn
Anger our huntsman: Breather round our farms
To keep off mildews, and all weather harms:
Strange ministrant of undescribed sounds,
That come a-swooning over hollow grounds,
And wither drearily on barren moors:
Dread opener of the mysterious doors
Leading to universal knowledge—see,
Great son of Dryope,
The many that are come to pay their vows
With leaves about their brows!

Be still the unimaginable lodge
For solitary thinkings; such as dodge
Conception to the very bourne of heaven,
Then leave the naked brain: be still the leaven,
That spreading in this dull and clodded earth
Gives it a touch ethereal—a new birth:
Be still a symbol of immensity;
A firmament reflected in a sea;
An element filling the space between;
An unknown—but no more: we humbly screen
With uplift hands our foreheads, lowly bending,
And giving out a shout most heaven rending,
Conjure thee to receive our humble pæan,
Upon thy Mount Lycean!

from ENDYMION

George Darley

1795–1846

From *SYLVIA, OR THE MAY QUEEN*

I

PEASANT SONG

O May, thou art a merry time,
    Sing hi! The hawthorn pink and pale!
When hedge-pipes they begin to chime,
    And summer flowers to sow the dale.

WHEN lasses and their lovers meet
    Beneath the early village morn,
And to the sound of tabor sweet
    Bid welcome to the maying morn!
      O May, etc.

When gray-beards and their gossips come
    With crutch in hand our sports to see,
And both go tottering, tattling home,
    Topful of wine as well as glee!
      O May, etc.

But youth was aye the time for bliss,
    So taste it, Shepherds! while ye may:
For who can tell that joy like this
    Will come another holiday?
      O May, thou art a merry time,
        Sing hi! The hawthorn pink and pale!
      When hedge-pipes they begin to chime,
        And summer flowers to sow the dale.

II

SONG OF THE GRACES

WE the Sun's bright daughters be!
    As our golden wings may show;
Every land and every sea
  Echoes our sweet ho-ran ho!
      Round, and round, and round we go
      Singing our sweet ho-ran ho!

Over heath, and over hill,
    Ho-ran, hi-ran, ho-ran ho!
At the wind's unruly will,
    Round, and round, and round we go.

Through the desert valley green,
    Ho-ran, etc.
Lonely mountain-cliffs between,
    Round, and round, etc.

Into cave and into wood,
    Ho-ran, etc.
Light as bubbles down the flood,
    Round, and round, etc.

By the many-tassell'd bower,
    Ho-ran, etc.
Nimming precious bosom-flower,
    Round, and round, etc.

Dimpling o'er the grassy meads,
    Ho-ran, etc.
Shaking gems from jewell'd heads,
    Round, and round, etc.

After bee, and after gnat,
>   *Ho-ran, etc.*
Hunting bird, and chasing bat,
>   *Round, and round, etc.*

Unto North, and unto South,
>   *Ho-ran, etc.*
In a trice to visit both,
>   *Round, and round, etc.*

To the East and to the West,
>   *Ho-ran, hi-ran, ho-ran ho!*
To the place that we love best.
>   *Round, and round, and round we go.*

From *SYREN SONGS*

I

THE SEA-RITUAL

PRAYER unsaid, and Mass unsung,
Deadman's dirge must still be rung:
>   *Dingle-dong,* the dead-bells sound!
Mermen chant his dirge around!

Wash him bloodless, smooth him fair,
Stretch his limbs, and sleek his hair:
>   *Dingle-dong,* the dead-bells go!
Mermen swing them to and fro!

In the wormless sand shall he
Feast for no foul glutton be:
>   *Dingle-dong,* the dead-bells chime!
Mermen keep the tone and time!

We must with a tombstone brave
Shut the shark out from his grave:
   Dingle-dong, the dead-bells toll!
   Mermen dirgers ring his knoll!

Such a slab will we lay o'er him,
All the dead shall rise before him:
   Dingle-dong, the dead-bells boom!
   Mermen lay him in his tomb!

II

THE MERMAIDENS' VESPER HYMN

TROOP home to silent grots and caves!
   Troop home! and mimic as you go
The mournful winding of the waves
Which to their dark abysses flow.

At this sweet hour, all things beside
In amorous pairs to covert creep:
The swans that brush the evening tide
Homeward in snowy couples keep.

In his green den the murmuring seal
Close by his sleek companion lies;
While singly we to bedward steal,
And close in fruitless sleep our eyes.

In bowers of love men take their rest,
In loveless bowers we sigh alone,
With bosom-friends are others blest—
But we have none! but we have none!

Thomas Hood
1799–1845

AUTUMN

I SAW old Autumn in the misty morn
  Stand shadowless like Silence, listening
To silence, for no lonely bird would sing
Into his hollow ear from woods forlorn,
Nor lowly hedge nor solitary thorn;—
Shaking his languid locks all dewy bright
With tangled gossamer that fell by night,
  Pearling his coronet of golden corn.

Where are the songs of Summer?—With the sun,
Oping the dusky eyelids of the south,
Till shade and silence waken up as one,
And Morning sings with a warm odorous mouth.
Where are the merry birds?—Away, away,
On panting wings through the inclement skies,
      Lest owls should prey
      Undazzled at noonday,
And tear with horny beak their lustrous eyes.

Where are the blooms of Summer?—In the west,
Blushing their last to the last sunny hours,
When the mild Eve by sudden Night is prest
Like tearful Proserpine, snatch'd from her flow'rs
      To a most gloomy breast.
Where is the pride of Summer,—the green prime,—
The many, many leaves all twinkling?—Three
On the moss'd elm; three on the naked lime
Trembling,—and one upon the old oak-tree!
  Where is the Dryad's immortality?—
Gone into mournful cypress and dark yew,

Or wearing the long gloomy Winter through
   In the smooth holly's green eternity.
The squirrel gloats on his accomplish'd hoard,
The ants have brimm'd their garners with ripe grain,
     And honey-bees have stored
The sweets of Summer in their luscious cells;
The swallows all have wing'd across the main;
And here the Autumn melancholy dwells,
    And sighs her tearful spells
Amongst the sunless shadows of the plain.
     Alone, alone,
       Upon a mossy stone,
She sits and reckons up the dead and gone
With the last leaves for a love-rosary,
Whilst all the wither'd world looks drearily,
Like a dim picture of the drownèd past
In the hush'd mind's mysterious far away,
Doubtful what ghostly thing will steal the last
Into that distance, gray upon the gray.

O go and sit with her, and be o'ershaded
Under the languid downfall of her hair:
She wears a coronal of flowers faded
Upon her forehead, and a face of care;—
There is enough of wither'd everywhere
To make her bower, and enough of gloom;
There is enough of sadness to invite,
If only for the rose that died, whose doom
Is Beauty's,—she that with the living bloom
Of conscious cheeks most beautifies the light:
There is enough of sorrowing, and quite
Enough of bitter fruits the earth doth bear,—
Enough of chilly droppings for her bowl;
Enough of fear and shadowy despair,
To frame her cloudy prison for the soul!
156

Thomas Lovell Beddoes

1803–1849

SONG FROM THE SHIP

TO sea, to sea! The calm is o'er;
  The wanton water leaps in sport,
And rattles down the pebbly shore;
The dolphin wheels, the sea-cows snort,
And unseen Mermaids' pearly song
Comes bubbling up, the weeds among.
  Fling broad the sail, dip deep the oar;
To sea, to sea! the calm is o'er.

To sea, to sea! our wide-winged bark
Shall billowy cleave its sunny way,
And with its shadow, fleet and dark,
Break the caved Tritons' azure day,
Like mighty eagle soaring light
O'er antelopes on Alpine height.
  The anchor heaves, the ship swings free,
The sails swell full: To sea, to sea!

from DEATH'S JEST-BOOK

Broadside and Street Ditties

I

THE MILKING-PAIL

YE nymphs and sylvan gods,
  That love green fields and woods,
When spring newly-born herself does adorn,
  With flowers and blooming buds:

Come sing in the praise, while flocks do graze,
  On yonder pleasant vale,
Of those that choose to milk their ewes,
And in cold dews, with clouted shoes,
  To carry the milking-pail.

  You goddess of the morn,
  With blushes you adorn,
And take the fresh air, whilst linnets prepare
  A concert on each green thorn;
The blackbird and thrush on every bush,
  And the charming nightingale,
In merry vein, their throats do strain
  To entertain the jolly train
  Of those of the milking-pail.

  When cold bleak winds do roar,
  And flowers will spring no more,
The fields that were seen so pleasant and green.
  With winter all candied o'er,
See now the town lass, with her white face,
  And her lips so deadly pale;
But it is not so, with those that go
Through frost and snow, with cheeks that glow,
  And carry the milking-pail.

  The country lad is free
  From fears and jealousy,
Whilst upon the green he oft is seen
  With his lass upon his knee.
With kisses so sweet he doth her so treat,
  And swears her charms won't fail;
But the London lass, in every place,
With brazen face, despises the grace
  Of those of the milking-pail.

Traditional version of a Broadside Ditty

II

OCH, JOHNNY, I HARDLY KNEW YE

WHILE going the road to sweet Athy,
  Hurroo! hurroo!
While going the road to sweet Athy,
  Hurroo! hurroo!
While going the road to sweet Athy,
A stick in my hand and a drop in my eye,
A doleful damsel I heard cry:
  "Och, Johnny, I hardly knew ye!
With drums and guns and guns and drums,
  The enemy nearly slew ye,
  My darling dear, you look so queer,
  Och, Johnny, I hardly knew ye!

"Where are your eyes that looked so mild?
  Hurroo! hurroo!
Where are your eyes that looked so mild?
  Hurroo! hurroo!
Where are your eyes that looked so mild
When my poor heart you first beguiled?
Why did you run from me and the child?
  Och, Johnny, I hardly knew ye!
With drums, etc.

"Where are the legs with which you run?
  Hurroo! hurroo!
Where are the legs with which you run?
  Hurroo! hurroo!
Where are the legs with which you run,
When you went to carry a gun?—
Indeed, your dancing days are done!
  Och, Johnny, I hardly knew ye!
With guns, etc.

159

"It grieved my heart to see you sail,
  Hurroo! hurroo!
It grieved my heart to see you sail,
  Hurroo! hurroo!
It grieved my heart to see you sail,
Though from my heart you took leg-bail,—
Like a cod you're doubled up head and tail.
  Och, Johnny, I hardly knew ye!
With guns, etc.

"You haven't an arm and you haven't a leg,
  Hurroo! hurroo!
You haven't an arm and you haven't a leg,
  Hurroo! hurroo!
You haven't an arm and you haven't a leg,
You're an eyeless, noseless, chickenless egg;
You'll have to be put in a bowl to beg;
  Och, Johnny, I hardly knew ye!
With guns, etc.

"I'm happy for to see you home,
  Hurroo! hurroo!
I'm happy for to see you home,
  Hurroo! hurroo!
I'm happy for to see you home,
All from the island of Sulloon,[1]
So low in flesh, so high in bone,
  Och, Johnny, I hardly knew ye!
With guns, etc.

"But sad as it is to see you so,
  Hurroo! hurroo!
But sad as it is to see you so,
  Hurroo! hurroo!

[1] Ceylon

But sad as it is to see you so,
And to think of you now as an object of woe,
Your Peggy'll still keep ye on as her beau;
   Och, Johnny, I hardly knew ye!
With drums and guns and guns and drums,
   The enemy nearly slew ye,
   My darling dear, you look so queer,
   Och, Johnny, I hardly knew ye!"

Traditional Irish Street Ballad

Elizabeth Barrett Browning

1806–1861

CHORUSES OF EDEN SPIRITS

*(Chanting from Paradise, while Adam and Eve fly
across the Sword-glare)*

SPIRITS OF THE TREES

HARK! the Eden trees are stirring,
   Soft and solemn in your hearing!
Oak and linden, palm and fir,
Tamarisk and juniper,
Each still throbbing in vibration
Since that crowning of creation
When the God-breath spake abroad,
Let us make man like to God!.
And the pine stood quivering
As the awful word went by,
Like a vibrant music-string
Stretched from mountain-peak to sky.
And the platan did expand
Slow and gradual, branch and head;

And the cedar's strong black shade
Fluttered brokenly and grand.
Grove and wood were swept aslant
In emotion jubilant.

VOICE OF THE SAME BUT SOFTER

Which divine impulsion cleaves
In dim movements to the leaves
Dropt and lifted, dropt and lifted
In the sunlight greenly sifted,—
In the sunlight and the moonlight
Greenly sifted through the trees.
Ever wave the Eden trees
In the nightlight and the noonlight,
With a ruffling of green branches
Shaded off to resonances,
Never stirred by rain or breeze.
 Fare ye well, farewell!
The sylvan sounds, no longer audible,
 Expire at Eden's door.
 Each footstep of your treading
Treads out some murmur which ye heard before.
 Farewell! the trees of Eden
 Ye shall hear nevermore.

RIVER-SPIRITS

Hark! the flow of the four rivers—
 Hark the flow!
How the silence round you shivers,
While our voices through it go,
 Cold and clear.

A SOFTER VOICE

Think a little, while ye hear,
 Of the banks
Where the willows and the deer
Crowd in intermingled ranks,

162

As if all would drink at once
Where the living water runs!—
Of the fishes' golden edges
Flashing in and out the sedges;
Of the swans on silver thrones,
Floating down the winding streams
With impassive eyes turned shoreward
And a chant of undertones,—
And the lotus leaning forward
To help them into dreams.
  Fare ye well, farewell!
The river-sounds, no longer audible,
  Expire at Eden's door.
  Each footstep of your treading
Treads out some murmur which ye heard before.
  Farewell! the streams of Eden,
  Ye shall hear nevermore.

BIRD-SPIRIT

I am the nearest nightingale
That singeth in Eden after you;
And I am singing loud and true,
And sweet,—I do not fail.
I sit upon a cypress bough,
Close to the gate, and I fling my song
Over the gate and through the mail
Of the warden angels marshalled strong,—
  Over the gate and after you!
And the warden angels let it pass,
Because the poor brown bird, alas,
  Sings in the garden, sweet and true.
And I build my song of high pure notes,
  Note over note, height over height,
  Till I strike the arch of the Infinite,

And I bridge abysmal agonies
With strong, clear calms of harmonies,—
And something abides, and something floats,
In the song which I sing after you.
　　Fare ye well, farewell!
The creature-sounds, no longer audible,
　　Expire at Eden's door.
　　Each footstep of your treading
Treads out some cadence which ye heard before.
　　Farewell! the birds of Eden,
　　Ye shall hear nevermore.

FLOWER-SPIRITS

We linger, we linger,
　　The last of the throng,
Like the tones of a singer
　　Who loves his own song.
We are spirit-aromas
　　Of blossom and bloom.
We call your thoughts home as
　　Ye breathe our perfume,—
To the amaranth's splendour
　　Afire on the slopes;
To the lily-bells tender,
　　And grey heliotropes;
To the poppy-plains keeping
　　Such dream-breath and blee
That the angels there stepping
　　Grew whiter to see:

　　　*　　*　　*　　*　　*

　　Fare ye well, farewell!
The Eden scents, no longer sensible,
　　Expire at Eden's door.

Each footstep of your treading
Treads out some fragrance which ye knew before.
Farewell! the flowers of Eden,
Ye shall smell nevermore.

from A DRAMA OF EXILE

John Greenleaf Whittier
1807–1892

SONG OF SLAVES IN THE DESERT

Where are we going? Where are we going,
Where are we going, Rubee?

LORD of peoples, lord of lands,
Look across these shining sands,
Through the furnace of the noon,
Through the white light of the moon.
Strong the Ghiblee wind is blowing,
Strange and large the world is growing!
Speak and tell us where we are going,
Where are we going, Rubee?

Bornou land was rich and good,
Wells of water, fields of food,
Dourra fields, and bloom of bean,
And the palm-tree cool and green:
Bornou land we see no longer,
Here we thirst and here we hunger,
Here the Moor-man smites in anger:
Where are we going, Rubee?

When we went from Bornou land,
We were like the leaves and sand,
We were many, we are few;
Life has one, and death has two:

Whitened bones our path are showing,
Thou All-seeing, thou All-knowing!
Hear us, tell us, where are we going,
   Where are we going, Rubee?

Moons of marches from our eyes
Bornou land behind us lies;
Stranger round us day by day
Bends the desert circle gray;
Wild the waves of sand are flowing,
Hot the winds above them blowing,—
Lord of all things!—where are we going?
   Where are we going, Rubee?

We are weak, but Thou art strong;
Short our lives, but Thine is long;
We are blind, but Thou hast eyes;
We are fools, but Thou art wise!
Thou, our morrow's pathway knowing
Through the strange world round us growing,
Hear us, tell us where are we going,
   Where are we going, Rubee?

Alfred, Lord Tennyson
1809–1892

CHORIC SONG

THERE is sweet music here that softer falls
   Than petals from blown roses on the grass,
Or night-dews on still waters between walls
Of shadowy granite, in a gleaming pass;
Music that gentlier on the spirit lies,

Than tir'd eyelids upon tir'd eyes;
Music that brings sweet sleep down from the blissful skies.
Here are cool mosses deep,
And thro' the moss the ivies creep,
And in the stream the long-leaved flowers weep,
And from the craggy ledge the poppy hangs in sleep.

Why are we weigh'd upon with heaviness,
And utterly consumed with sharp distress,
While all things else have rest from weariness?
All things have rest: why should we toil alone,
We only toil, who are the first of things,
And make perpetual moan,
Still from one sorrow to another thrown:
Nor ever fold our wings,
And cease from wanderings,
Nor steep our brows in slumber's holy balm;
Nor harken what the inner spirit sings,
"There is no joy but calm!"
Why should we only toil, the roof and crown of things?

Lo! in the middle of the wood,
The folded leaf is woo'd from out the bud
With winds upon the branch, and there
Grows green and broad, and takes no care,
Sun-steep'd at noon, and in the moon
Nightly dew-fed; and turning yellow
Falls, and floats adown the air.
Lo! sweeten'd with the summer light,
The full-juiced apple, waxing over-mellow,
Drops in a silent autumn night.
All its allotted length of days,
The flower ripens in its place,
Ripens and fades, and falls, and hath no toil,
Fast-rooted in the fruitful soil.

Hateful is the dark blue sky,
Vaulted o'er the dark-blue sea.
Death is the end of life; ah, why
Should life all labour be?
Let us alone. Time driveth onward fast,
And in a little while our lips are dumb.
Let us alone. What is it that will last?
All things are taken from us, and become
Portions and parcels of the dreadful Past.
Let us alone. What pleasure can we have
To war with evil? Is there any peace
In ever climbing up the climbing wave?
All things have rest, and ripen toward the grave
In silence; ripen, fall and cease:
Give us long rest or death, dark death, or dreamful ease.

How sweet it were, hearing the downward stream,
With half-shut eyes ever to seem
Falling asleep in a half-dream!
To dream and dream, like yonder amber light,
Which will not leave the myrrh-bush on the height;
To hear each other's whisper'd speech;
Eating the Lotos day by day,
To watch the crisping ripples on the beach,
And tender curving lines of creamy spray;
To lend our hearts and spirits wholly
To the influence of mild-minded melancholy;
To muse and brood and live again in memory,
With those old faces of our infancy
Heap'd over with a mound of grass,
Two handfuls of white dust, shut in an urn of brass!

Dear is the memory of our wedded lives,
And dear the last embraces of our wives

And their warm tears: but all hath suffer'd change:
For surely now our household hearths are cold:
Our sons inherit us: our looks are strange:
And we should come like ghosts to trouble joy.
Or else the island princes over-bold
Have eat our substance, and the minstrel sings
Before them of the ten years' war in Troy,
And our great deeds, as half-forgotten things.
Is there confusion in the little isle?
Let what is broken so remain.
The Gods are hard to reconcile:
'Tis hard to settle order once again.
There *is* confusion worse than death,
Trouble on trouble, pain on pain,
Long labour unto aged breath,
Sore task to hearts worn out by many wars
And eyes grown dim with gazing on the pilot-stars.

But, propt on beds of amaranth and moly,
How sweet (while warm airs lull us, blowing lowly)
With half-dropt eyelid still,
Beneath a heaven dark and holy,
To watch the long bright river drawing slowly
His waters from the purple hill—
To hear the dewy echoes calling
From cave to cave thro' the thick-twined vine—
To watch the emerald-colour'd water falling
Thro' many a wov'n acanthus-wreath divine!
Only to hear and see the far-off sparkling brine,
Only to hear were sweet, stretch'd out beneath the pine.

The Lotos blooms below the barren peak:
The Lotos blows by every winding creek:
All day the wind breathes low with mellower tone:
Thro' every hollow cave and alley lone

Round and round the spicy downs the yellow Lotos-dust is
blown.
We have had enough of action, and of motion we,
Roll'd to starboard, roll'd to larboard, when the surge was
seething free,
Where the wallowing monster spouted his foam-fountains
in the sea.
Let us swear an oath, and keep it with an equal mind,
In the hollow Lotos-land to live and lie reclined
On the hills like Gods together, careless of mankind.
For they lie beside their nectar, and the bolts are hurl'd
Far below them in the valleys, and the clouds are lightly
curl'd
Round their golden houses, girdled with the gleaming world:
Where they smile in secret, looking over wasted lands,
Blight and famine, plague and earthquake, roaring deeps
and fiery sands,
Clanging fights, and flaming towns, and sinking ships, and
praying hands.
But they smile, they find a music centred in a doleful song
Steaming up, a lamentation and an ancient tale of wrong,
Like a tale of little meaning tho' the words are strong;
Chanted from an ill-used race of men that cleave the soil,
Sow the seed, and reap the harvest with enduring toil,
Storing yearly little dues of wheat, and wine and oil;
Till they perish and they suffer—some, 'tis whisper'd—
down in hell
Suffer endless anguish, others in Elysian valleys dwell,
Resting weary limbs at last on beds of asphodel.
Surely, surely, slumber is more sweet than toil, the shore
Than labour in the deep mid-ocean, wind and wave and
oar;
Oh rest ye, brother mariners, we will not wander more.

from THE LOTOS EATERS

CLARIBEL

A Melody

WHERE Claribel low-lieth
   The breezes pause and die,
  Letting the rose-leaves fall:
But the solemn oak-tree sigheth,
   Thick-leaved, ambrosial,
  With an ancient melody
  Of an inward agony,
Where Claribel low-lieth.

At eve the beetle boometh
  Athwart the thicket lone:
At noon the wild bee hummeth
  About the moss'd headstone:
At midnight the moon cometh,
  And looketh down alone.
Her song the lintwhite swelleth,
The clear-voiced mavis dwelleth,
  The callow throstle lispeth,
The slumbrous wave outwelleth,
  The babbling runnel crispeth,
The hollow grot replieth
  Where Claribel low-lieth.

Robert Browning

1812–1889

CAVALIER TUNES

I

MARCHING ALONG

KENTISH Sir Byng stood for his King,
   Bidding the crop-headed Parliament swing:
And, pressing a troop unable to stoop
And see the rogues flourish and honest folk droop,
Marched them along, fifty-score strong,
Great-hearted gentlemen, singing this song.

God for King Charles! Pym and such carles
To the Devil that prompts 'em their treasonous parles!
Cavaliers, up! Lips from the cup,
Hands from the pasty, nor bite take nor sup
Till you're—
  (*Cho.*) *Marching along, fifty-score strong,*
     Great-hearted gentlemen, singing this song.

Hampden to Hell, and his obsequies' knell
Serve Hazelrig, Fiennes, and young Harry as well!
England, good cheer! Rupert is near!
Kentish and loyalists, keep we not here
  (*Cho.*) *Marching along, fifty-score strong,*
     Great-hearted gentlemen, singing this song!

Then, God for King Charles! Pym and his snarls
To the Devil that pricks on such pestilent carles!
Hold by the right, you double your might;
So, onward to Nottingham, fresh for the fight,
   (*Cho.*) *March we along, fifty-score strong,*
        Great-hearted gentlemen, singing this song!

II

GIVE A ROUSE

KING CHARLES, and who'll do him right now?
   King Charles, and who's ripe for fight now?
Give a rouse: here's, in Hell's despite now,
King Charles!

Who gave me the goods that went since?
Who raised me the house that sank once?
Who helped me to gold I spent since?
Who found me in wine you drank once?

   (*Cho.*) *King Charles, and who'll do him right now?*
        King Charles, and who's ripe for fight now?
        Give a rouse: here's, in Hell's despite now,
        King Charles!

To whom used my boy George quaff else,
By the old fool's side that begot him?
For whom did he cheer and laugh else,
While Noll's damned troopers shot him?

   (*Cho.*) *King Charles, and who'll do him right now?*
        King Charles, and who's ripe for fight now?
        Give a rouse: here's, in Hell's despite now,
        King Charles!

James Russell Lowell

1819–1891

From *THE PRESENT CRISIS*

WHEN a deed is done for Freedom, through the
    broad earth's aching breast
Runs a thrill of joy prophetic, trembling on from east to
    west,
And the slave, where'er he cowers, feels the soul within him
    climb
To the awful verge of manhood, as the energy sublime
Of a century bursts full-blossomed on the thorny stem of
    Time.

*　*　*　*　*

Backward look across the ages and the beacon-moments see,
That, like peaks of some sunk continent, jut through
    Oblivion's sea;
Not an ear in court or market for the low foreboding cry
Of those Crises, God's stern winnowers, from whose feet
    earth's chaff must fly;
Never shows the choice momentous till the judgment hath
    passed by.

Careless seems the great Avenger; history's pages but record
One death-grapple in the darkness twixt old systems and
    the Word;
Truth forever on the scaffold, Wrong forever on the throne,
Yet that scaffold sways the future, and, behind the dim
    unknown,
Standeth God within the shadow, keeping watch above His
    own.

*　*　*　*　*

174

For Humanity sweeps onward: where to-day the martyr
    stands,
On the morrow crouches Judas with the silver in his hands;
Far in front the cross stands ready and the crackling fagots
    burn,
While the hooting mob of yesterday in silent awe return
To glean up the scattered ashes into History's golden urn.

*   *   *   *   *

New occasions teach new duties; Time makes ancient good
    uncouth;
They must upward still, and onward, who would keep
    abreast of Truth;
Lo, before us gleam her camp-fires! we ourselves must Pil-
    grims be,
Launch our Mayflower, and steer boldly through the des-
    perate winter sea,
Nor attempt the Future's portal with the Past's blood-rusted
    key.

Walt Whitman

1819–1892

MIRACLES

WHY, who makes much of a miracle?
    As to me I know of nothing else but miracles,
Whether I walk the streets of Manhattan,
Or dart my sight over the roofs of houses towards the sky,
Or wade with naked feet along the beach just in the edge of
    the water,
Or stand under trees in the woods,
Or talk by day with any one I love, or sleep in the bed at
    night with any one I love,
Or sit at table at dinner with the rest,

Or look at strangers opposite me riding in the car,
Or watch honey-bees busy around the hive of a summer
    forenoon,
Or animals feeding in the fields,
Or birds, or the wonderfulness of insects in the air,
Or the wonderfulness of the sundown, or of stars shining so
    quiet and bright,
Or the exquisite delicate thin curve of the new moon in
    spring;
These with the rest, one and all, are to me miracles,
The whole referring, yet each distinct and in its place.

To me every hour of the light and dark is a miracle,
Every cubic inch of space is a miracle,
Every square yard of the surface of the earth is spread with
    the same,
Every foot of the interior swarms with the same.

To me the sea is a continual miracle,
The fishes that swim—the rocks—the motion of the waves—
    the ships with men in them,
What stranger miracles are there?

SONG FOR ALL SEAS, ALL SHIPS

I

TO-DAY a rude brief recitative,
    Of ships sailing the seas, each with its special flag or
    ship-signal,
Of unnamed heroes in the ships—of waves spreading and
    spreading far as the eye can reach,
Of dashing spray, and the winds piping and blowing,
And out of these a chant for the sailors of all nations,
Fitful, like a surge.

Of sea-captains young or old, and the mates, and of all
 intrepid sailors,
Of the few, very choice, taciturn, whom fate can never sur-
 prise nor death dismay,
Pick'd sparingly without noise by thee, old ocean, chosen by
 thee,
Thou sea that pickest and cullest the race in time, and
 unitest nations,
Suckled by thee, old husky nurse, embodying thee,
Indomitable, untamed as thee.

(Ever the heroes on water or on land, by ones or twos
 appearing,
Ever the stock preserv'd and never lost, though rare, enough
 for seed preserv'd.)

II

Flaunt out O sea your separate flags of nations!
Flaunt out visible as ever the various ship-signals!
But do you reserve especially for yourself and for the soul
 of man one flag above all the rest,
A spiritual woven signal for all nations, emblem of man
 elate above death,
Token of all brave captains and all intrepid sailors and mates,
And all that went down doing their duty,
Reminiscent of them, twined from all intrepid captains
 young or old,
A pennant universal, subtly waving all time, o'er all brave
 sailors,
All seas, all ships.

BEAT! BEAT! DRUMS

BEAT! beat! drums!—blow! bugles! blow!
Through the windows—through doors—burst like a
 ruthless force,

M

Into the solemn church, and scatter the congregation,
Into the school where the scholar is studying;
Leave not the bridegroom quiet—no happiness must he
have now with his bride,
Nor the peaceful farmer any peace, ploughing his field or
gathering his grain,
So fierce you whirr and pound you drums—so shrill you
bugles blow.

Beat! beat! drums!—blow! bugles! blow!
Over the traffic of cities—over the rumble of wheels in the
streets;
Are beds prepared for sleepers at night in the houses? no
sleepers must sleep in those beds,
No bargainers' bargains by day—no brokers or speculators
—would they continue?
Would the talkers be talking? would the singer attempt to
sing?
Would the lawyer rise in the court to state his case before
the judge?
Then rattle quicker, heavier drums—you bugles wilder
blow.

Beat! beat! drums!—blow! bugles! blow!
Make no parley—stop for no expostulation,
Mind not the timid—mind not the weeper or prayer,
Mind not the old man beseeching the young man,
Let not the child's voice be heard, nor the mother's en-
treaties,
Make even the trestles to shake the dead where they lie
awaiting the hearses,
So strong you thump O terrible drums—so loud you bugles
blow.

O CAPTAIN! MY CAPTAIN!

(On the death of Abraham Lincoln)

O CAPTAIN! my Captain! our fearful trip is done,
   The ship has weather'd every rack, the prize we
   sought is won,
The port is near, the bells I hear, the people all exulting,
While follow eyes the steady keel, the vessel grim and
    daring;
        But O heart! heart! heart!
        O the bleeding drops of red,
           Where on the deck my Captain lies,
           Fallen cold and dead.

O Captain! my Captain! rise up and hear the bells;
Rise up—for you the flag is flung—for you the bugle trills,
For you bouquets and ribbon'd wreaths—for you the shores
    a-crowding,
For you they call, the swaying mass, their eager faces
    turning;
        Here Captain! dear father!
        This arm beneath your head!
          It is some dream that on the deck
          You've fallen cold and dead.

My Captain does not answer, his lips are pale and still,
My father does not feel my arm, he has no pulse nor will,
The ship is anchor'd safe and sound, its voyage closed and
    done,
From fearful trip the victor ship comes in with object won;
        Exult O shores, and ring O bells!
        But I with mournful tread,
          Walk the deck my Captain lies
          Fallen cold and dead.

Matthew Arnold

1822–1888

DESIRE

THOU, who dost dwell alone—
    Thou, who dost know thine own—
Thou, to whom all are known
From the cradle to the grave—
    Save, oh, save.
From the world's temptations,
    From tribulations;
From that fierce anguish
Wherein we languish;
From that torpor deep
Wherein we lie asleep,
Heavy as death, cold as the grave;
    Save, oh, save.

When the Soul, growing clearer,
    Sees God no nearer:
When the Soul, mounting higher,
    To God comes no nigher:
But the arch-fiend Pride
Mounts at her side,
Foiling her high emprize,
Sealing her eagle eyes,
And, when she fain would soar,
Makes idols to adore;
Changing the pure emotion
Of her high devotion,
To a skin-deep sense
Of her own eloquence:
Strong to deceive, strong to enslave—
    Save, oh, save.

From the ingrain'd fashion
Of this earthly nature
That mars thy creature.
From grief, that is but passion;
From mirth, that is but feigning;
From tears, that bring no healing;
From wild and weak complaining;
   Thine old strength revealing,
      Save, oh, save.
From doubt, where all is double:
Where wise men are not strong:
Where comfort turns to trouble:
Where just men suffer wrong:
Where sorrow treads on joy:
Where sweet things soonest cloy:
Where faiths are built on dust:
Where Love is half mistrust,
Hungry, and barren, and sharp as the sea;
      Oh, set us free.
O let the false dream fly
Where our sick souls do lie
   Tossing continually.
O where thy voice doth come
   Let all doubts be dumb:
   Let all words be mild:
   All strifes be reconcil'd:
   All pains beguil'd.
Light bring no blindness;
Love no unkindness;
Knowledge no ruin;
Fear no undoing.
From the cradle to the grave,
    Save, oh, save.

Dante Gabriel Rossetti

1828–1882

CHIMES

I

HONEY-FLOWERS to the honey-comb
And the honey-bee's from home.

A honey-comb and a honey-flower,
And the bee shall have his hour.

A honeyed heart for the honey-comb,
And the humming bee flies home.

A heavy heart in the honey-flower,
And the bee has had his hour.

II

A honey cell's in the honeysuckle,
And the honey-bee knows it well.

The honey-comb has a heart of honey,
And the humming bee's so bonny.

A honey-flower's the honeysuckle,
And the bee's in the honey-bell.

The honeysuckle is sucked of honey,
And the bee is heavy and bonny.

III

Brown shell first for the butterfly
And a bright wing by and by.

Butterfly, good-bye to your shell,
And, bright wings, speed you well.

Bright lamplight for the butterfly
And a burnt wing by and by.

Butterfly, alas for your shell,
And, bright wings, fare you well.

IV

Lost love-labour and lullaby,
And lowly let love lie.

Lost love-morrow and love-fellow
And love's life lying low.

Lovelor labour and life laid by
And lowly let love lie.

Late love-longing and life-sorrow
And love's life lying low.

V

Beauty's body and benison
With a bosom-flower new blown.

Bitter beauty and blessing bann'd
With a breast to burn and brand.

Beauty's bower in the dust o'erblown
With a bare white breast of bone.

Barren beauty and bower of sand
With a blast on either hand.

VI

Buried bars in the breakwater
And bubble of the brimming weir.

Body's blood in the breakwater
And a buried body's bier.

Buried bones in the breakwater
And bubble of the brawling weir.

Bitter tears in the breakwater
And a breaking heart to bear.

VII

Hollow heaven and the hurricane
And hurry of the heavy rain.

Hurried clouds in the hollow heaven
And a heavy rain hard-driven.

The heavy rain it hurries amain
And heaven and the hurricane.

Hurrying wind o'er the heaven's hollow
And the heavy rain to follow.

William Morris
1834–1894

From *THE LIFE AND DEATH OF JASON*

I

SONG OF ORPHEUS FOR THE ARGONAUTS

O BITTER sea, tumultuous sea,
   Full many an ill is wrought by thee!—
Unto the wasters of the land
   Thou holdest out thy wrinkled hand;

And when they leave the conquered town
Whose black smoke makes thy surges brown,
Driven betwixt thee and the sun,
As the long day of blood is done,
From many a league of glittering waves
Thou smilest on them and their slaves.
 The thin bright-eyed Phœnician
Thou drawest to thy waters wan:
With ruddy eve and golden morn
Thou temptest him, until, forlorn,
Unburied, under alien skies,
Cast up ashore his body lies.

 Yea, whoso sees thee at his door,
Must ever long for more and more;
Nor will the beechen bowl suffice,
Or homespun robe of little price,
Or hood well-woven of the fleece
Undyed, or unspiced wine of Greece;
So sore his heart is set upon
Purple, and gold, and cinnamon;
For as thou cravest, so he craves,
Until he rolls beneath thy waves.
Nor in some landlocked unknown bay
Can satiate thee for one day.

 Now, therefore, O thou bitter sea,
With no long words we pray to thee,
But ask thee, hast thou felt before
Such strokes of the long ashen oar?
And hast thou yet seen such a prow
Thy rich and niggard waters plough?

 Nor yet, O sea, shalt thou be cursed,
If at thy hands we gain the worst,
And, wrapt in water, roll about
Blind-eyed, unheeding song or shout,
Within thine eddies far from shore,

Warmed by no sunlight any more.
  Therefore, indeed, we joy in thee,
And praise thy greatness, and will we
Take at thy hands both good and ill,
Yea, what thou wilt, and praise thee still,
Enduring not to sit at home,
And wait until the last days come,
When we no more may care to hold
White bosoms under crowns of gold,
And our dull hearts no longer are
Stirred by the clangorous noise of war,
And hope within our souls is dead,
And no joy is rememberèd.
  So, if thou hast a mind to slay,
Fair prize thou hast of us to-day;
And if thou hast a mind to save,
Great praise and honour shalt thou have:
But whatso thou wilt do with us,
Our end shall not be piteous,
Because our memories shall live
When folk forget the way to drive
The black keel through the heaped-up sea,
And half dried up thy waters be.

II

SONG OF THE HESPERIDES

O YE, who to this place have strayed,
    That never for man's eyes was made,
Depart in haste, as ye have come,
And bear back to your sea-beat home

This memory of the age of gold,
And for your eyes, grown overbold,
Your hearts shall pay in sorrowing,
For want of many a half-seen thing.

Lo, such as is this garden green,
In days past, all the world has been,
And what we know all people knew,
Save this, that unto worse all grew.
But since the golden age is gone,
This little place is left alone,
Unchanged, unchanging, watched of us,
The daughters of wise Hesperus.
Surely the heavenly Messenger
Full oft is fain to enter here,
And yet without must he abide;
Nor longeth less the dark king's bride
To set red lips unto that fruit
That erst made nought her mother's suit.
Here would Diana rest awhile,
Forgetful of her woodland guile,
Among these beasts that fear her nought.
Nor is it less in Pallas' thought,
Beneath our trees to ponder o'er
The wide unfathomed sea of lore;
And oft-kissed Citheræa, no less
Weary of love, full fain would press
These flowers with soft unsandalled feet.

But unto us our rest is sweet,
Neither shall any man or God
Or lovely Goddess touch the sod
Where-under old times buried lie,
Before the world knew misery.

Nor will we have a slave or king,
Nor yet will we learn anything
But what we know, that makes us glad;
While oft the very Gods are sad
With knowing what the Fates shall do.
 Neither from us shall wisdom go
To fill the hungering hearts of men,
Lest to them threescore years and ten
Come but to seem a little day,
Once given, and taken soon away.
Nay, rather let them find their life
Bitter and sweet, fulfilled of strife,
Restless with hope, vain with regret,
Trembling with fear, most strangely set
'Twixt memory and forgetfulness;
So more shall joy be, troubles less,
And surely when all else is past,
They shall not want their rest at last.

 Let earth and heaven go their way,
While still we watch from day to day,
In this green place left all alone,
A remnant of the days long gone.

from THE LIFE AND DEATH OF JASON

SONG OF THE YOUNG MEN AND GIRLS TO VENUS

BEFORE our lady came on earth
Little there was of joy or mirth;
About the borders of the sea
The sea-folk wandered heavily;
About the wintry river side
The weary fishers would abide.

Alone within the weaving-room
The girls would sit before the loom,
And sing no song, and play no play;
Alone from dawn to hot mid-day,
From mid-day unto evening,
The men afield would work, nor sing,
'Mid weary thoughts of man and God,
Before thy feet the wet ways trod.

Unkissed the merchant bore his care,
Unkissed the knights went out to war,
Unkissed the mariner came home,
Unkissed the minstrel men did roam.

Or in the stream the maids would stare,
Nor know why they were made so fair;
Their yellow locks, their bosoms white,
Their limbs well wrought for all delight,
Seemed foolish things that waited death,
As hopeless as the flowers beneath
The weariness of unkissed feet:
No life was bitter then, or sweet.

Therefore, O Venus, well may we
Praise the green ridges of the sea
O'er which, upon a happy day,
Thou cam'st to take our shame away.
Well may we praise the curdling foam
Amidst the which thy feet did bloom,
Flowers of the gods; the yellow sand
They kissed atwixt the sea and land;
The bee-beset ripe-seeded grass,
Through which thy fine limbs first did pass;

The purple-dusted butterfly,
First blown against thy quivering thigh;
The first red rose that touched thy side,
And over-blown and fainting died;
The flickering of the orange shade,
Where first in sleep thy limbs were laid;
The happy day's sweet life and death,
Whose air first caught thy balmy breath—
Yea, all these things well praised may be,
But with what words shall we praise thee—
O Venus, O thou love alive,
Born to give peace to souls that strive?

from THE HILL OF VENUS

THE BURGHERS' BATTLE

THICK rise the spear-shafts o'er the land
 That erst thy harvest bore;
The sword is heavy in the hand,
And we return no more.
The light wind waves the Ruddy Fox,
Our banner of the war,
And ripples in the Running Ox,
And we return no more.
Across our stubble acres now
The teams go four and four;
But out-worn elders guide the plough,
And we return no more.
And now the women heavy-eyed
Turn through the open door
From gazing down the highway wide,
Where we return no more.
The shadows of the fruited close

Dapple the feast-hall floor;
There lie our dogs and dream and doze,
And we return no more.
Down from the minster tower to-day
Fall the soft chimes of yore
Amidst the chattering jackdaws' play:
And we return no more.
But underneath the streets are still;
Noon, and the market's o'er!
Back go the goodwives o'er the hill;
For we return no more.
What merchant to our gates shall come?
What wise man bring us lore?
What abbot ride away to Rome,
Now we return no more?
What mayor shall rule the hall we built?
Whose scarlet sweep the floor?
What judge shall doom the robber's guilt,
Now we return no more?
New houses in the street shall rise
Where builded we before,
Of other stone wrought otherwise;
For we return no more.
And crops shall cover field and hill
Unlike what once they bore,
And all be done without our will,
Now we return no more.
Look up! the arrows streak the sky,
The horns of battle roar;
The long spears lower and draw nigh,
And we return no more.
Remember how beside the wain,
We spoke the word of war,
And sowed this harvest of the plain,
And we return no more.

Lay spears about the Ruddy Fox!
The days of old are o'er;
Heave sword about the Running Ox!
For we return no more.

THE TWO SIDES OF THE RIVER

THE YOUTHS

O WINTER, O white winter, wert thou gone,
No more within the wilds were I alone,
Leaping with bent bow over stock and stone!

No more alone my love the lamp should burn,
Watching the weary spindle twist and turn,
Or o'er the web hold back her tears and yearn:
O winter, O white winter, wert thou gone!

THE MAIDENS

Sweet thoughts fly swiftlier than the drifting snow,
And with the twisting threads sweet longings grow,
And o'er the web sweet pictures come and go,
For no white winter are we long alone.

THE YOUTHS

O stream so changed, what hast thou done to me,
That I thy glittering ford no more can see
Wreathing with white her fair feet lovingly?

See, in the rain she stands, and, looking down
With frightened eyes upon thy whirlpools brown,
Drops to her feet again her girded gown.
O hurrying turbid stream, what hast thou done?

192

THE MAIDENS

The clouds lift, telling of a happier day
When through the thin stream I shall take my way,
Girt round with gold, and garlanded with may,
What rushing stream can keep us long alone?

THE YOUTHS

O burning Sun, O master of unrest,
Why must we, toiling, cast away the best,
Now, when the bird sleeps by her empty nest?
See, with my garland lying at her feet,
In lonely labour stands mine own, my sweet,
Above the quern half-filled with half-ground wheat.
O red taskmaster, that thy flames were done!

THE MAIDENS

O love, to-night across the half-shorn plain
Shall I not go to meet the yellow wain,
A look of love at end of toil to gain?
What flaming sun can keep us long alone?

THE YOUTHS

To-morrow, said I, is grape gathering o'er;
To-morrow, and our loves are twinned no more.
To-morrow came, to bring us woes and war.

What have I done, that I should stand with these
Hearkening the dread shouts borne upon the breeze,
While she, far off, sits weeping 'neath her trees?
Alas, O kings, what is it ye have done?

THE MAIDENS

Come, love, delay not; come, and slay my dread!
Already is the banquet table spread;

In the cool chamber flower-strewn is my bed:
Come, love, what king shall keep us long alone?

THE YOUTHS

O city, city, open thou thy gate!
See, with life snatched from out the hand of fate,
How on thy glittering triumph I must wait!

Are not her hands stretched out to me? Her eyes,
Grow they not weary as each new hope dies,
And lone before her still the long road lies?
O golden city, fain would I be gone!

THE MAIDENS

And thou art happy, amid shouts and songs,
And all that unto conquering men belongs.
Night hath no fear for me, and day no wrongs.
What brazen city gates can keep us, lone?

THE YOUTHS

O long, long road, how bare thou art, and grey!
Hill after hill thou climbest, and the day
Is ended now, O moonlit endless way!

And she is standing where the rushes grow,
And still with white hand shakes her anxious brow,
Though 'neath the world the sun is fallen now,
O dreary road, when will thy leagues be done?

THE MAIDENS

O tremblest thou, grey road, or do my feet
Tremble with joy, thy flinty face to meet?
Because my love's eyes soon mine eyes shall greet?
No heart thou hast to keep us long alone.

194

THE YOUTHS

O wilt thou ne'er depart, thou heavy night?
When will thy slaying bring on the morning bright,
That leads my weary feet to my delight?

Why lingerest thou, filling with wandering fears
My lone love's tired heart; her eyes with tears
For thoughts like sorrow for the vanished years?
Weaver of ill thoughts, when wilt thou be gone?

THE MAIDENS

Love, to the east are thine eyes turned as mine,
In patient watching for the night's decline?
And hast thou noted this grey widening line?
Can any darkness keep us long alone?

THE YOUTHS

O day, O day, is it a little thing
That thou so long unto thy life must cling,
Because I gave thee such a welcoming?

I called thee king of all felicity,
I praised thee that thou broughtest joy so nigh;
Thine hours are turned to years, thou will not die;
O day so longed for, would that thou wert gone!

THE MAIDENS

The light fails, love; the long day soon shall be
Nought but a pensive happy memory
Blessed for the tales it told to thee and me.
How hard it was, O love, to be alone.

Algernon Charles Swinburne
1837–1909

From *THE LITANY OF NATIONS*

Chorus

IF with voice of words or prayers thy sons may reach thee,
   We thy latter sons, the men thine after-birth.
We the children of thy grey-grown age, O Earth,
O our mother everlasting, we beseech thee.
By the sealed and secret ages of thy life;
  By the darkness wherein grew thy sacred forces;
  By the songs of stars thy sisters in their courses;
By thine own song hoarse and hollow and shrill with strife;
By thy voice distuned and marred of modulation;
  By the discord of thy measure's march with theirs;
  By the beauties of thy bosom, and the cares;
By thy glory of growth, and splendour of thy station;
By the shame of men thy children, and the pride;
  By the pale-cheeked hope that sleeps and weeps and
    passes,
  As the grey dew from the morning mountain-grasses;
By the white-lipped sightless memories that abide;

    *   *   *   *   *

By thy morning and thine evening, night and day;
  By the first white light that stirs and strives and hovers
  As a bird above the brood her bosom covers,
By the sweet last star that takes the westward way;
By the night whose feet are shod with snow or thunder,
  Fledged with plumes of storm, or soundless as the dew;
  By the vesture bound of many-folded blue
Round her breathless breasts, and all the woven wonder;

By the golden-growing eastern stream of sea;
　By the sounds of sunrise moving in the mountains;
　By the forces of the floods and unsealed fountains;
Thou that badest man be born, bid man be free.

Greece

I am she that made thee lovely with my beauty
　　From north to south:
Mine, the fairest lips, took first the fire of duty
　　From thine own mouth.
Mine, the fairest eyes, sought first thy laws and knew them
　　Truths undefiled;
Mine, the fairest hands, took freedom first into them,
　　A weanling child.
By my light, now he lies sleeping, seen above him
　　Where none sees other;
By my dead that loved and living men that loved him;
　　(*Chor.*) *Hear us, O mother.*

Italy

I am she that was the light of thee enkindled
　　When Greece grew dim;
She whose life grew up with man's free life, and dwindled
　　With wane of him.
She that once by sword and once by word imperial
　　Struck bright thy gloom;
And a third time, casting off these years funereal,
　　Shall burst thy tomb.
By that bond 'twixt thee and me whereat affrighted
　　Thy tyrants fear us;
By that hope and this remembrance reunited;
　　(*Chor.*) *O mother, hear us.*

Spain

I am she that set my seal upon the nameless
    West worlds of seas;
And my sons as brides took unto them the tameless
    Hesperides.
Till my sins and sons through sinless lands dispersèd,
    With red flame shod,
Made accurst the name of man, and thrice accursèd
    The name of God.
Lest for those past fires the fires of my repentance
    Hell's fume yet smother,
Now my blood would buy remission of my sentence;
    (Chor.) Hear us, O mother.

France

I am she that was thy sign and standard-bearer,
    Thy voice and cry;
She that washed thee with her blood and left thee fairer,
    The same was I.
Were not these the hands that raised thee fallen and fed thee,
    These hands defiled?
Was not I thy tongue that spake, thine eye that led thee,
    Not I thy child?
By the darkness on our dreams, and the dead errors
    Of dead times near us;
By the hopes that hang around thee, and the terrors;
    (Chor.) O mother, hear us.

Russia

I am she whose hands are strong and her eyes blinded
    And lips athirst
Till upon the night of nations many-minded
    One bright day burst:

198

Till the myriad stars be molten into one light,
    And that light thine;
Till the soul of man be parcel of the sunlight,
    And thine of mine.
By the snows that blanch not him nor cleanse from slaughter
    Who slays his brother;
By the stains and by the chains on me thy daughter;
    (*Chor.*) *Hear us, O mother.*

Switzerland

I am she that shews on mighty limbs and maiden
    Nor chain nor stain;
For what blood can touch these hands with gold unladen,
    These feet what chain?
By the surf of spears one shieldless bosom breasted
    And was my shield,
Till the plume-plucked Austrian vulture-heads twin-crested
    Twice drenched the field;
By the snows and souls untrampled and untroubled
    That shine to cheer us,
Light of those to these responsive and redoubled;
    (*Chor.*) *O mother, hear us.*

Germany

I am she beside whose forest-hidden fountains
    Slept freedom armed,
By the magic born to music in my mountains
    Heart-chained and charmed.
By those days the very dream whereof delivers
    My soul from wrong;
By the sounds that make of all my ringing rivers
    None knows what song;
By the many tribes and names of my division
    One from another;
By the single eye of sun-compelling vision;
    (*Chor.*) *Hear us, O mother.*

England

I am she that was and was not of thy chosen,
　　　　　Free, and not free;
She that fed thy springs, till now her springs are frozen;
　　　　　Yet I am she.
By the sea that clothed and sun that saw me splendid
　　　　　And fame that crowned,
By the song-fires and the sword-fires mixed and blended
　　　　　That robed me round;
By the star that Milton's soul for Shelley's lighted,
　　　　　Whose rays insphere us;
By the beacon-bright Republic far-off sighted;
　　　　　(*Chor.*) *O mother, hear us.*

Chorus

Turn away from us the cross-blown blasts of error,
　　　　　That drown each other;
Turn away the fearful cry, the loud-tongued terror,
　　　　　O Earth, O mother.
Turn away their eyes who track, their hearts who follow,
　　　　　The pathless past;
Shew the soul of man, as summer shews the swallow,
　　　　　The way at last.
By the sloth of men who all too long endure men
　　　　　On man to tread;
By the cry of men, the bitter cry of poor men,
　　　　　That faint for bread;

* 　 * 　 * 　 * 　 *

By the pastures that give grass to feed the lamb in,
　　　　　Where men lack meat;
By the cities clad with gold and shame and famine;
　　　　　By field and street;

200

By the people, by the poor man, by the master
       That men call slave;
By the cross-winds of defeat and of disaster,
       By wreck, by wave;
By the helm that keeps us still to sunwards driving,
       Still eastward bound,
Till, as night-watch ends, day burn on eyes reviving,
       And land be found:
We thy children, that arraign not nor impeach thee
       Though no star steer us,
By the waves that wash the morning we beseech thee,
       O mother, hear us.

from SONGS BEFORE SUNRISE

From *WINTER IN NORTHUMBERLAND*

(*Songs of Four Seasons*)

OUTSIDE the garden
   The wet skies harden;
The gates are barred on
  The summer side;
"Shut out the flower-time,
Sunbeam and shower-time;
Make way for our time,"
  Wild winds have cried.
Green once and cheery
The woods, worn weary,
Sigh as the dreary
  Weak sun goes home:
A great wind grapples
The wave, and dapples
The dead green floor of the sea with foam.

Through fell and moorland,
And salt-sea foreland,
Our noisy norland
   Resounds and rings;
Waste waves thereunder
Are blown in sunder,
And winds make thunder
   With cloudwide wings;
Sea-drift makes dimmer
The beacon's glimmer;
Nor sail nor swimmer
   Can try the tides;
And snowdrifts thicken
Where, when leaves quicken,
Under the heather the sundew hides.

Green land and red land,
Moorside and headland,
Are white as dead land,
   Are all as one;
Nor honied heather,
Nor bells to gather,
Fair with fair weather
   And faithful sun:
Fierce frost has eaten
All flowers that sweeten
The fells rain-beaten;
   And winds their foes
Have made the snow's bed
Down in the rose-bed;
Deep in the snow's bed bury the rose.

*   *   *   *   *

Each reed that grows in
Our stream is frozen,
The fields it flows in
  Are hard and black;
The water-fairy
Waits wise and wary
Till time shall vary
  And thaws come back.
"O sister, water,"
The wind besought her,
"O twin-born daughter
  Of spring with me,
Stay with me, play with me,
Take the warm way with me,
Straight for the summer and oversea."

But winds will vary,
And wise and wary
The patient fairy
  Of water waits;
All shrunk and wizen,
In iron prison,
Till spring re-risen
  Unbar the gates;
Till, as with clamour
Of axe and hammer,
Chained streams that stammer
  And struggle in straits
Burst bonds that shiver,
And thaws deliver
The roaring river in stormy spates.

In fierce March weather
White waves break tether,

And whirled together
   At either hand,
Like weeds uplifted,
The tree-trunks rifted
In spars are drifted,
   Like foam or sand,
Past swamp and sallow
And reed-beds callow,
Through pool and shallow,
   To wind and lee,
Till, no more tongue-tied,
Full flood and young tide
Roar down the rapids and storm the sea.

   As men's cheeks faded
On shores invaded,
When shorewards waded
   The lords of fight;
When churl and craven
Saw hard on haven
The wide-winged raven
   At mainmast height;
When monks affrighted
To windward sighted
The birds full-flighted
   Of swift sea-kings;
So earth turns paler
When Storm the sailor
Steers in with a roar in the race of his wings.

   O strong sea-sailor,
Whose cheek turns paler
For wind or hail or
   For fear of thee?

O far sea-farer,
O thunder-bearer,
Thy songs are rarer
   Than soft songs be.
O fleet-foot stranger,
O north-sea ranger
Through days of danger
   And ways of fear,
Blow thy horn here for us,
Blow the sky clear for us,
Send us the song of the sea to hear.

Roll the strong stream of it
Up, till the scream of it
Wake from a dream of it
   Children that sleep,
Seamen that fare for them
Forth, with a prayer for them;
Shall not God care for them,
     Angels not keep?
Spare not the surges
Thy stormy scourges;
Spare us the dirges
   Of wives that weep.
Turn back the waves for us:
Dig no fresh graves for us,
Wind, in the manifold gulfs of the deep.

O stout north-easter,
Sea-king, land-waster,
For all thy haste, or
   Thy stormy skill,

Yet hadst thou never,
For all endeavour,
Strength to dissever
    Or strength to spill,
Save for his giving
Who gave our living,
Whose hands are weaving
    What ours fulfil;
Whose feet tread under
The storms and thunder,
Who made our wonder to work his will.

His years and hours,
His world's blind powers,
His stars and flowers,
    His nights and days,
Sea-tide and river,
And waves that shiver,
Praise God, the giver
    Of tongues to praise.
Winds in their blowing,
And fruits in growing;
Time in its going,
    While time shall be;
In death and living,
With one thanksgiving,
Praise Him whose hand is the strength of the sea.

from POEMS AND BALLADS: SERIES II

TRIADS

THE word of the sun to the sky,
    The word of the wind to the sea,
The word of the moon to the night,
        What may it be?

The sense to the flower of the fly,
   The sense of the bird to the tree,
      The sense to the cloud of the light,
         Who can tell me?

The song of the fields to the kye,
   The song of the lime to the bee,
      The song of the depth to the height,
         Who knows all three?

from POEMS AND BALLADS: SERIES II

From *Prelude to* TRISTRAM OF LYONESSE

LOVE, that is first and last of all things made,
   The light that has the living world for shade,
The spirit that for temporal veil has on
The souls of all men woven in unison,
One fiery raiment with all lives inwrought
And lights of sunny and starry deed and thought,
And alway through new act and passion new
Shines the divine same body and beauty through,
The body spiritual of fire and light
That is to worldly noon as noon to night;
Love, that is flesh upon the spirit of man
And spirit within the flesh whence breath began;
Love, that keeps all the choir of lives in chime;
Love, that is blood within the veins of time;
That wrought the whole world without stroke of hand,
Shaping the breadth of sea, the length of land,
And with the pulse and motion of his breath
Through the great heart of earth strikes life and death,
The sweet twain chords that make the sweet tune live
Through day and night of things alternative,
Through silence and through sound of stress and strife,
And ebb and flow of dying death and life;

207

Love, that sounds loud or light in all men's ears,
Whence all men's eyes take fire from sparks of tears,
That binds on all men's feet or chains or wings;
Love, that is root and fruit of terrene things;
Love, that the whole world's waters shall not drown,
The whole world's fiery forces not burn down;
Love, that what time his own hands guard his head
The whole world's wrath and strength shall not strike dead;
Love, that if once his own hands make his grave
The whole world's pity and sorrow shall not save;
Love, that for very life shall not be sold,
Nor bought nor bound with iron nor with gold;
So strong that heaven, could love bid heaven farewell,
Would turn to fruitless, and unflowering hell;
So sweet that hell, to hell could love be given,
Would turn to splendid and sonorous heaven;
Love that is fire within thee and light above,
And lives by grace of nothing but of love;
Through many and lovely thoughts and much desire
Led these twain to the life of tears and fire;
Through many and lovely days and much delight
Led these twain to the lifeless life of night.

* * * * *

They have the night, who had like us the day;
We, whom day binds, shall have the night as they.
We, from the fetters of the light unbound,
Healed of our wound of living, shall sleep sound.

* * * * *

Us too, when all the tears of time are dry,
The night shall lighten from her tearless eye.
Blind is the day and eyeless all its light,
But the large unbewildered eye of night
208

Hath sense and speculation; and the sheer
Limitless length of lifeless life and clear;
The timeless space wherein the brief worlds move
Clothed with light life and fruitful with light love,
With hopes that threaten, and with fears that cease,
Past fear and hope, hath in it only peace.

CHORUS FROM ERECHTHEUS

(First three Strophes and two Antistrophes)

Strophe 1

WHO shall put a bridle in the mourner's lips to chasten
    them,
Or seal up the fountains of his tears for shame?
Song nor prayer nor prophecy shall slacken tears nor hasten
   them,
  Till grief be within him as a burnt-out flame;
     Till the passion be broken in his breast
     And the might thereof molten into rest,
    And the rain of eyes that weep be dry,
    And the breath be stilled of lips that sigh.

Antistrophe 1

Death at last for all men is harbour; yet they flee from it,
  Set sails to the storm-wind and again to sea;
Yet for all their labour no whit further shall they be from it,
  Nor longer but wearier shall their life's work be.
     And with anguish of travail until night
     Shall they steer into shipwreck out of sight,
    And with oars that break and shrouds that strain
    Shall they drive whence no ship steers again.

Strophe 2

Bitter and strange is the word of the God most high,
      And steep the strait of his way.
Through a pass rock-rimmed and narrow the light that
    gleams
On the faces of men falls faint as the dawn of dreams,
The dayspring of death as a star in an under sky
      Where night is the deadmen's day.

Antistrophe 2

As darkness and storm is his will that on earth is done,
      As a cloud is the face of his strength.
King of kings, holiest of holies, and mightiest of might,
Lord of lords of thine heaven that are humble in thy sight,
Hast thou set not an end for the path of the fires of the sun,
      To appoint him a rest at length?

Strophe 3

Hast thou told not by measure the waves of the waste wide
    sea,
And the ways of the wind their master and thrall to thee?
   Hast thou filled not the furrows with fruit for the world's
    increase?
Has thine ear not heard from of old or thine eye not read
The thought and the deed of us living, the doom of us dead?
   Hast thou not made war upon earth, and again made
    peace?
Therefore, O Father, that seest us whose lives are a breath,
Take off us thy burden, and give us not wholly to death.

Thomas Hardy

1840–1928

CHORUSES ON THE EVE OF WATERLOO

The focus of the scene follows the retreating English army, the highway and its margins panoramically gliding past the vision of the spectator. The phantoms chant monotonously while the retreat goes on.

CHORUS OF RUMOURS (*aerial music*)

DAY'S nether hours advance; storm supervenes
   In heaviness unparalleled, that screens
With water-woven gauzes, vapour-bred,
The creeping clumps of half-obliterate red—
Severely harassed past each round and ridge
By the inimical lance. They gain the bridge
And village of Genappe, in equal fence
With weather and the enemy's violence.
—Cannon upon the foul and flooded road,
Cavalry in the cornfields mire-bestrowed,
With frothy horses floundering to their knees,
Make wayfaring a moil of miseries!
Till Britishry and Bonapartists lose
Their clashing colours for the tawny hues
That twilight sets on all its stealing tinct imbues.

The rising ground of Mont Saint-Jean, in front of Waterloo, is gained by the English vanguard and main masses of foot, and by degrees they are joined by the cavalry and artillery. The French are but little later in taking up their position amid the cornfields around La Belle Alliance.

Fires begin to shine up from the English bivouacs. Camp kettles are slung, and the men pile arms and stand round the blaze to dry themselves. The French opposite lie down like

211

dead men in the dripping green wheat and rye, without supper and without fire.

By and by the English army also lies down, the men huddling together on the ploughed mud in their wet blankets, while some sleep sitting round the dying fires.

CHORUS OF THE YEARS (*aerial music*)

The eyelids of eve fall together at last,
And the forms so foreign to field and tree
Lie down as though native, and slumber fast!

CHORUS OF THE PITIES

Sore are the thrills of misgiving we see
In the artless champaign at this harlequinade,
Distracting a vigil where calm should be!

The green seems opprest, and the Plain afraid
Of a Something to come, whereof these are the proofs,—
Neither earthquake, nor storm, nor eclipse's shade!

CHORUS OF THE YEARS

Yea, the coneys are scared by the thud of hoofs,
And their white scuts flash at their vanishing heels,
And swallows abandon the hamlet-roofs.

The mole's tunnelled chambers are crushed by wheels,
The lark's eggs scattered, their owners fled;
And the hedgehog's household the sapper unseals.

The snail draws in at the terrible tread,
But in vain; he is crushed by the felloe-rim;
The worm asks what can be overhead,
212

And wriggles deep from a scene so grim,
And guesses him safe; for he does not know
What a foul red flood will be soaking him!

Beaten about by the heel and toe
Are butterflies, sick of the day's long rheum,
To die of a worse than the weather-foe.

Trodden and bruised to a miry tomb
Are ears that have greened but will never be gold,
And flowers in the bud that will never bloom.

CHORUS OF THE PITIES

So the season's intent, ere its fruit unfold,
Is frustrate, and mangled, and made succumb,
Like a youth of promise struck stark and cold! . . .

And what of these who to-night have come?

CHORUS OF THE YEARS

The young sleep sound; but the weather awakes
In the veterans, pains from the past that numb;

Old stabs of Ind, old Peninsular aches,
Old Friedland chills, haunt their moist mud bed,
Cramps from Austerlitz; till their slumber breaks.

CHORUS OF SINISTER SPIRITS

And each soul shivers as he shifts his head
On the loam he's to lease with the other dead
From to-morrow's mist-fall till Time be sped!

The fires of the English go out, and silence prevails, save for the soft hiss of the rain that falls impartially on both the sleeping armies.

from THE DYNASTS

213

Gerard Manley Hopkins
1844–1898

THE LEADEN ECHO AND
THE GOLDEN ECHO

(*Maidens' Song from St Winefred's Well*)

THE LEADEN ECHO

HOW to kéep—is there ány any, is there none such,
nowhere known some, bow or brooch or braid or brace,
láce, latch or catch or key to keep
Back beauty, keep it, beauty, beauty, beauty, . . . from
vanishing away?
Ó is there no frowning of these wrinkles, rankèd wrinkles
deep,
Dówn? no waving off of these most mournful messengers,
still messengers, sad and stealing messengers of grey?
No there's none, there's none, O no there's none,
Nor can you long be, what you now are, called fair,
Do what you may do, what, do what you may,
And wisdom is early to despair:
Be beginning; since, no, nothing can be done
To keep at bay
Age and age's evils, hoar hair,
Ruck and wrinkle, drooping, dying, death's worst, winding
sheets, tombs and worms and tumbling to decay;
So be beginning, be beginning to despair.
O there's none; no no no there's none:
Be beginning to despair, to despair,
Despair, despair, despair, despair.

214

Spare!

There is one, yes I have one (Hush there!);

Only not within seeing of the sun,

Not within the singeing of the strong sun,

Tall sun's tingeing, or treacherous the tainting of the earth's
air,

Somewhere elsewhere there is ah well where! one,

One. Yes I can tell such a key, I do know such a place,

Where whatever's prized and passes of us, everything that's
fresh and fast flying of us, seems to us sweet of us and
swiftly away with, done away with, undone,

Undone, done with, soon done with, and yet dearly and
dangerously sweet

Of us, the wimpled-water-dimpled, not-by-morning-
matchèd face,

The flower of beauty, fleece of beauty, too too apt to, ah!
to fleet,

Never fleets móre, fastened with the tenderest truth

To its own best being and its loveliness of youth: it is an
everlastingness of, O it is an all youth!

Come then, your ways and airs and looks, locks, maiden
gear, gallantry and gaiety and grace,

Winning ways, airs innocent, maiden manners, sweet looks,
loose locks, long locks, lovelocks, gaygear, going gallant, girlgrace—

Resign them, sign them, seal them, send them, motion them
with breath,

And with sighs soaring, soaring síghs deliver

Them; beauty-in-the-ghost, deliver it, early now, long
before death

Give beauty back, beauty, beauty, beauty, back to God,
beauty's self and beauty's giver.

See; not a hair is, not an eyelash, not the least lash lost;
every hair

Is, hair of the head, numbered.
Nay, what we had lighthanded left in surly the mere mould
Will have waked and have waxed and have walked with the
      wind what while we slept,
This side, that side hurling a heavyheaded hundredfold
What while we, while we slumbered.
O then, weary then whý should we tread? O why are we so
      haggard at the heart, so care-coiled, care-killed, so
      fagged, so fashed, so cogged, so cumbered,
When the thing we freely fórfeit is kept with fonder a care,
Fonder a care kept than we could have kept it, kept
Far with fonder a care (and we, we should have lost it)
      finer, fonder
A care kept.—Where kept? Do but tell us where kept,
      where.—
Yonder.—What high as that! We follow, now we follow.—
      Yonder, yes yonder, yonder,
Yonder.

Robert Bridges

1844–1930

CHORUS OF SCYRIAN MAIDENS

THE earth loveth the spring,
   Nor of her coming despaireth,
Withheld by nightly sting,
Snow, and icy fling,
The snarl of the North:
But nevertheless she prepareth
And setteth in order her nurslings to bring them forth.
   The jewels of her delight,
   What shall be blue, what yellow or white;
   What softest above the rest,

The primrose, that loveth best
    Woodland skirts and the copses shorn.
And on the day of relenting she suddenly weareth
Her budding crowns. O then, in the early morn,
    Is any song that compareth
With the gaiety of birds, that thrill the gladdened air
    In exhaustible chorus
    To awake the sons of the soil
With music more than in brilliant halls sonorous
    (—It cannot compare—)
    Is fed to the ears of kings
    From the reeds and hirèd strings?
    For love maketh them glad;
    And if a soul be sad,
    Or a heart oracle dumb,
Here may it taste the promise of joy to come.

For the Earth knoweth the love which made her.
    The omnipotent one desire,
    Which burns at her heart like fire,
    And hath in gladness arrayed her.
    And man with the Maker shareth,
    Him also to rival throughout the lands,
    To make a work with his hands
    And have his children adore it:
The Creator smileth on him who is wise and dareth
    In understanding with pride:
For God, where'er he hath builded, dwelleth wide,—
    And he careth,—
    To set a task to the smallest atom,
    The law-abiding grains,
    That hearken each and rejoice:
For he guideth the world as a horse with reins;
    It obeyeth his voice
And lo! he hath set a beautiful end before it:

Whereto it leapeth and striveth continually,
And pitieth nought, nor spareth:
The mother's wail for her children slain,
The stain of disease,
The darts of pain,
The waste of the fruits of trees,
The slaughter of cattle,
Unbrotherly lust, the war
Of hunger, blood, and the yells of battle,
It heedeth no more
Than a carver regardeth the wood that he cutteth away:
The grainèd shavings fall at his feet,
But that which his tool hath spared shall stand
For men to praise the work of his hand;
For he cutteth so far, and there it lay,
And his work is complete.

But I will praise 'mong men the masters of mind
In music and song,
Who follow the love of God to bless their kind:
And I pray they find
A marriage of mirth—
And a life long
With the gaiety of the Earth.

from ACHILLES IN SCYROS

CHORUS OF OCEANIDES

I (*a*)

BRIGHT day succeedeth unto day—
Night to pensive night—
With his towering ray
Of all-fathering light—
With the solemn trance
Of her starry dance.—

Nought is new or strange
In the eternal change.—

As the light clouds fly
O'er the tree-tops high,
So the days go by.—

Ripples that arrive
On the sunny shore,
Dying to their live
Music evermore.—

Like pearls on a thread,—
Like notes of a song,—
Like the measur'd tread
Of a dancing throng.—

(b)

Ocëanides are we,
  Nereids of the foam,
But we left the sea
On the earth to roam
With the fairest Queen
That the world hath seen.—

Why amidst our play
Was she sped away?—

Over hill and plain
We have sought in vain;
She comes not again.—

Not the Naiads knew
On their dewy lawns:—
Not the laughing crew
Of the leaping Fauns.—

Now, since she is gone,
All our dance is slow,
All our joy is done,
And our song is woe.—

from DEMETER

John Davidson

1857–1909

SONG OF A TRAIN

A MONSTER taught
To come to hand
Amain,
As swift as thought across the land
The train.

The song it sings
Has an iron sound;
Its iron wings
Like wheels go round.

Crash under bridges,
Flash over ridges,
And vault the downs;
The road is straight—
Nor stile, nor gate;
For milestones—towns!

Voluminous, vanishing, white,
The steam plume trails;
Parallel streaks of light,
The polished rails.

Oh, what can follow?
The little swallow,
The trout of the sky:
But the sun
Is outrun,
And Time passed by.

O'er bosky dens,
By marsh and mead,
Forest and fens,
Embodied speed
Is clanked and hurled;
O'er rivers and runnels;
And into the earth
And out again
In death and birth
That know no pain,
For the whole round earth
Is a warren of railway tunnels

Hark! hark! hark!
It screams and cleaves the dark;
And the subterranean night
Is gilt with smoky light.
Then out again apace
It runs its thundering race,
The monster taught
To come to hand
Amain,
That swift as thought
Speeds through the land,
The train.

PIPER, PLAY!

NOW the furnaces are out,
  And the aching anvils sleep;
Down the road the grimy rout
  Tramples homeward twenty deep.
    Piper, play! Piper, play!
      Though we be o'erlaboured men,
      Ripe for rest, pipe your best!
      Let us foot it once again!

Bridled looms delay their din;
  All the humming wheels are spent;
Busy spindles cease to spin;
  Warp and woof must rest content.
    Piper, play! Piper, play!
      For a little we are free!
      Foot it girls and shake your curls,
        Haggard creatures though we be!

Racked and soiled the faded air
  Freshens in our holiday;
Clouds and tides our respite share;
  Breezes linger by the way.
    Piper, rest! Piper, rest!
      Now, a carol of the moon!
      Piper, piper, play your best!
      Melt the sun into your tune!

We are of the humblest grade;
  Yet we dare to dance our fill:
Male and female were we made—
  Fathers, mothers, lovers still!
    Piper—softly; soft and low;
      Pipe of love in mellow notes,
      Till the tears begin to flow,
        And our hearts are in our throats!

Nameless as the stars of night
 Far in galaxies unfurled,
Yet we wield unrivalled might,
 Joints and hinges of the world!
  Night and day! night and day!
   Sound the song the hours rehearse!
  Work and play! work and play!
   The order of the universe!

Now the furnaces are out,
 And the aching anvils sleep;
Down the road a merry rout
 Dances homeward, twenty deep.
  Piper, play! Piper, play!
   Wearied people though we be,
  Ripe for rest, pipe your best!
   For a little we are free!

Francis Thompson

1859–1907

THE MAKING OF VIOLA

I

The Father of Heaven
        SPIN, daughter Mary, spin,
         Twirl your wheel with silver din;
        Spin, daughter Mary, spin,
         Spin a tress for Viola.
Angels

        Spin, Queen Mary, a
        Brown tress for Viola!

The Father of Heaven
> Weave, hands angelical,
> Weave a woof of flesh to pall—
> Weave, hands angelical—
> > Flesh to pall our Viola.

Angels

> Weave, singing brothers, a
> Velvet flesh for Viola!

The Father of Heaven
> Scoop, young Jesus, for her eyes,
> Wood-browned pools of Paradise—
> Young Jesus, for the eyes,
> > For the eyes of Viola.

Angels

> Tint, Prince Jesus, a
> Duskèd eye for Viola!

The Father of Heaven
> Cast a star therein to drown,
> Like a torch in cavern brown,
> Sink a burning star to drown
> > Whelmed in eyes of Viola.

Angels

> Lave, Prince Jesus, a
> Star in eyes of Viola!

The Father of Heaven
> Breathe, Lord Paraclete,
> To a bubbled crystal meet—
> Breathe, Lord Paraclete—
> > Crystal soul for Viola.

224

Angels
>Breathe, Regal Spirit, a
>Flashing soul for Viola!

VI

The Father of Heaven
>Child-angels, from your wings
>Fall the roseal hoverings,
>Child-angels, from your wings,
>>On the cheeks of Viola.

Angels
>Linger, rosy reflex, a
>Quenchless stain, on Viola!

VII

All things being accomplished, saith the Father of Heaven,
>Bear her down, and bearing, sing,
>Bear her down on spyless wing,
>Bear her down, and bearing, sing,
>>With a sound of viola.

Angels
>Music as her name is, a
>Sweet sound of Viola!

VIII

>Wheeling angels, past espial,
>Danced her down with sound of viol;
>Wheeling angels, past espial,
>>Descanting on "Viola."

Angels
>Sing, in our footing, a
>Lovely lilt of "Viola!"

P

Baby smiled, mother wailed,
Earthward while the sweetling sailed;
Mother smiled, baby wailed,
When to earth came Viola.

And her elders shall say:
So soon have we taught you a
Way to weep, poor Viola!

Smile, sweet baby, smile,
For you will have weeping-while;
Native in your Heaven is smile,—
But your weeping, Viola?

Whence your smiles we know, but ah!
Whence your weeping, Viola?—
Our first gift to you is a
Gift of tears, my Viola!

SONG OF THE HOURS

SCENE: Before the Palace of the Sun, into which a god has just passed as the guest of Hyperion. TIME: Dawn. The Hours of Night and Day advance on each other as the gates close.

MORNING HOURS

IN curbed expanses our wheeling dances
Meet from the left and right;
Under this vaporous awning
Tarrying awhile in our flight,

Waiting the day's advances,
  We, the children of light,
Clasp you on verge of the dawning,
  Sisters of Even and Night!

CHORUS

We who lash from the way of the sun
  With the whip of the winds the thronging clouds
Who puff out the lights of the stars, or run
  To scare dreams back to their shrouds,
Or tiar the temples of Heaven
  With a crystalline gleam of showers;

EVENING HOURS

While to flit with the soft moth, Even,
  Round the lamp of the day is ours;

NIGHT HOURS

And ours with her crescent argentine,
  To make Night's forehead fair,
To wheel up her throne of the earth, and twine
  The daffodils in her hair;

ALL

  We, moulted as plumes are,
From the wings whereon Time is borne;

MORNING HOURS

We, buds who in blossoming foretell
  The date when our leaves shall be torn;

NIGHT HOURS

We, knowing our dooms are to plunge with the gloom's car
  Down the steep ruin of morn;

227

We hail thee, Immortal!
We robes of Life, mouldering while worn.

NIGHT HOURS

Sea-birds, winging o'er sea calm-strewn
  To the lure of the beacon-stars, are we,
O'er the foamy wake of the white-sailed moon,
  Which to men is the Galaxy.

MORNING HOURS

Our eyes, through our pinions folden,
  By the filtered flame are teased
As we bow when the sun makes golden
  Earthquake in the East.

EVENING HOURS

And *we* shake on the sky a dusted fire
  From the ripened sunset's anther,
While the flecked main, drowsing in gorged desire,
  Purrs like an outstretched panther.

MORNING HOURS

O'er the dead moon-maid
  We draw softly the day's white pall;
And our children the Moments we see as
  In drops of the dew they fall,
Or on light plumes laid they shoot the cascade
  Of colours some Heaven's bow call;

ALL

And we sing, Guest, to thee, as
Thou pacest the crystal-paved hall!

We, while the sun with his hid chain swings
  Like a censer around him the blossom-sweet earth,

Who dare the lark with our passionate wings,
    And its mirth with our masterless mirth;
    Or—when that flying laughter
        Has sunk and died away
    Which beat against Heaven's rafter—
        Who vex the clear eyes of day,
Who weave for the sky in the loom of the cloud
    A mantle of waving rain,
We, whose hair is jewelled with joys, or bowed
    Under veilings of misty pain;
    We hymn thee at leaving
Who strew thy feet's coming, O Guest!
    We, the linked cincture which girdles
Mortality's feverous breast,
Who heave in its heaving, who grieve in its grieving,
    Are restless in its unrest;
Our beings unstirred else
    Were it not for the bosom they pressed.

We see the wind, like a light swift leopard
    Leap on the flocks of the cloud that flee,
As we follow the feet of the radiant shepherd
    Whose bright sheep drink of the sea.
    When that drunken Titan the Thunder
        Stumbles through staggered Heaven,
    And spills on the scorched earth under
        The fiery wine of the levin,
With our mystic measure of rhythmic motion
    We charm him in snorting sleep,
While round him the sun enchants from ocean
    The walls of a cloudy keep.
    Beneath the deep umbers
Of night as we watch and hark,
    The dim-wingèd dreams which feed on
The blossoms of day we mark,

As in numerous numbers they swarm to the slumbers
 That cell the hive of the dark;
And life shakes, a reed on
 Our tide, in the death-wind stark.

Time, Eternity's fountain, whose waters
 Fall back thither from whence they rose,
Deweth with us, its showery daughters,
 The Life that is green in its flows.
But whether in grief or mirth we shower,
 We make not the thing we breed,
For what may come of the passing Hour
 Is what was hid in the seed.
  And now as wakes,
   Like love in its first blind guesses,
  Or a snake just stirring its coils,
   Sweet tune into half-caresses,
  Before the sun shakes the clinging flakes
   Of gloom from his spouting tresses,
  Let winds have toils
   To catch at our fluttering dresses!
Winter, that numbeth the throstle and stilled wren,
 Has keen frost-edges our plumes to pare,
Till we break, with the Summer's laughing children,
 Over the fields of air.
   While the winds in their tricksome courses
    The snowy steeds vault upon
   That are foaled of the white sea-horses
    And washed in the streams of the sun.
Thaw, O thaw the enchanted throbbings
 Curdled at Music's heart;
Tread she her grapes till from their englobings
 The melodies spurt and smart!
   We fleet as a rain,
    Nor yearn for the being men own,

With whom is naught beginneth
  Or endeth without some moan;
We soar to our zenith
  And are panglessly overblown.

Yet, if the roots of the truth were bare,
  Our transcience is only a mortal seeming;
Fond men, we are fixed as a still despair,
  And we fleet but in your dreaming.
  We are columns in Time's hall, mortals,
    Wherethrough Life hurrieth;
  You pass in at birth's wide portals,
    And out at the postern of death.
As you chase down the vista your dream or your love
  The swift pillars race you by,
And you think it is we who move, who move,—
  It is you who die, who die!
  O firmament, even
    You pass, by whose fixture man voweth;
  God breathes you forth as a bubble
    And shall suck you back into His mouth!
  Through earth, sea, and Heaven a doom shall be driven,
    And, sown in the furrows it plougheth,
  As fire bursts from stubble
    Shall spring the new wonders none troweth.

The bowed East lifteth the dripping sun,
  A golden cup, to the lips of Night,
Over whose cheeks in flushes run
  The heats of the liquid light.

MORNING HOURS

To our very pinions' ridge
  We tremble expectantly;—

231

Is it ready, the burnished bridge
　　　We must cast for our King o'er the sea?
And who will kneel with sunbeam-slips
　　To dry the flowers' sweet eyes?
Who touch with fire her finger-tips
　　For the lamp of the grape, as she flies?

ALL

　List, list to the prances, his chariot advances,
　　It comes in a dust of light!
　From under our brightening awning
　We wheel in a diverse flight:
Yet the hands we unclasp, as our dances
　Sweep off to the left and the right,
Are but loosed on the verge of the dawning
　To join on the verge of the night.

NEW YEAR'S CHIMES

WHAT is the song the stars sing?
　　(And a million songs are as song of one)
This is the song the stars sing:
　(Sweeter song's none)

One to set, and many to sing,
　(And a million songs are as song of one
One to stand, and many to cling,
The many things, and the one Thing,
　The one that runs not, the many that run.

232

The ever new weaveth the ever old,
  (*And a million songs are as song of one*)
Ever telling the never told;
The silver saith, and the said is gold,
  And done ever the never done.

The chase that's chased is the Lord o' the chase,
  (*And a million songs are as song of one*)
And the pursued cries on the race;
  And the hounds in leash are the hounds that run

Hidden stars by the shown stars' sheen;
  (*And a million suns are but as one*)
Colours unseen by the colours seen,
And sounds unheard heard sounds between,
  And a night is in the light of the sun.

An ambuscade of light in night,
  (*And a million secrets are but as one*)
And a night is dark in the sun's light,
  And a world in the world man looks upon.

Hidden stars by the shown stars' wings,
  (*And a million cycles are but as one*)
And a world with unapparent strings
Knits the simulant world of things;
  Behold, and vision thereof is none.

The world above in the world below,
  (*And a million worlds are but as one*)
And the One in all; as the sun's strength so
Strives in all strength, glows in all glow
  Of the earth that wits not, and man thereon.

Braced in its own fourfold embrace
  (*And a million strengths are as strength of one*)
And round it all God's arms of grace,
The world, so as the Vision says,
    Doth with great lightning-tramples run.

And thunder bruiteth into thunder,
  (*And a million sounds are as sound of one*)
From stellate peak to peak is tossed a voice of wonder,
And the height stoops down to the depths thereunder,
    And sun leans forth to his brother-sun.

And the more ample years unfold
  (*With a million songs as song of one*)
A little new of the ever old,
A little told of the never told,
    Added act of the never done.

Loud the descant, and low the theme,
  (*A million songs are as song of one*)
And the dream of the world is dream in dream,
But the one Is is, or naught could seem;
    And the song runs round to the song begun.

This is the song the stars sing,
  (*Tonèd all in time*)
Tintinnabulous, tuned to ring
A multitudinous-single thing
  (*Rung all in rhyme*).

Sir Henry Newbolt

1862–1938

O PULCHRITUDO

O SAINT whose thousand shrines our feet have trod
　　And our eyes loved thy lamp's eternal beam,
Dim earthly radiance of the Unknown God,
　　Hope of the darkness, light of them that dream,
Far off, far off and faint, O glimmer on
Till we thy pilgrims from the road are gone.

O Word whose meaning every sense hath sought,
　　Voice of the teeming field and grassy mound,
Deep-whispering fountain of the wells of thought,
　　Will of the wind and soul of all sweet sound,
Far off, far off and faint, O murmur on
Till we thy children from the road are gone.

William Butler Yeats

1865–1939

A FAERY SONG

*Sung by the people of Faery over Diarmuid
and Grania, in their bridal sleep
under a Cromlech*

WE who are old, old and gay,
　　O so old!
Thousands of years, thousands of years,
If all were told:

Give to these children, new from the world,
Silence and love;
And the long dew-dropping hours of the night,
And the stars above:

Give to these children, new from the world,
Rest far from men.
Is anything better, anything better?
Tell us it then:

Us who are old, old and gay,
O so old!
Thousands of years, thousands of years,
If all were told.

Laurence Binyon

1869–1943

From *THE SIRENS*

SING the Finders! Sing the bold
Trusters of Earth, those patient ones,
That listen to the subtle words
Of Silence in the streams and stones;
Ponderers of the secret-souled
Bodies quick with ignorant being;
Followers of the clues that thread
Differences and accords;
Wooers of what powers agreeing
May the hands of man bestead;
Seers who have turned aside

From the greeds that ask and ache
Blinded to all else beside,—
Letting the clear spirit take
Truth from vision open-eyed.
Breaks the bud for him that sees
In a world of promises.

Sing the breaker of the dark,
Sing the finder of the flame,
Troubler of the essential spark
Lurking in the withered pith
Or from stony prison freed,
Friend and fury, holy need
And fierce destroyer, hard to tame,
Risen, a God to wrestle with!
Sing the bender of the wheel,
Mother of the shapes of speed!
Sing the launcher of the keel
Carrying thought's arrow-aim
Beyond the sundown,—sowing seed
Of man on coasts untrod before,
To widen memory's haunted shore
And add the nearness of a name.

Far-descended old desire!
That stirred in swarming forest-ages,
Prowled by fear whose stealthy eye
Watched from glooms, where hunger-rages
Ravened; see at last the Hand
Emerging human, stretched to try
Shapes of things with wondering pleasure,
When its strength forgets to kill;
Tempted on to understand,
Serving ways of secret will,—
Fit and fashion, poise and measure.

Sing the hand that builds the wall
And spans the river, and arches over
Man the worshipper and lover
Song-like stone; the hand so strong
To strike, yet in whose touch is all
Life's mystery that wooes from things
Their strength, as music from the strings,—
Touch of the mind that seeks behind
The world for the befriending Mind.
Sing the openers of the gates!
Sing the changers of the fates!
Sing the seekers! them that saw,
Past the seeming starry roof
Of human earth, in mazy plan
Bright eternities of law;
Them that neared those orbs to man,
Unafraid, and put to proof
Divination's ancient scheme;
Stept into the timeless stream,
Star-like spirits among the stars!
Sing the seekers! Chosen souls,
Grapnel'd in the very marrow
By a thought that night and day
Draws them whither their unknown
Mighty lover far away
Beckons them to the frore Poles
Or new meridians; like to him
Who climbed in Panama the tree,
And splendour of untravelled sea
Smote him like a glorious arrow:
Never shall he rest again
Till he sail that virgin main!
Or like him who quietly
Sitting in his Polar tent
Found so great a way to die;

Hope-forsaken, famine-spent,
Wrote his words of faith and cheer
Till the pen dropt from the hand
That wrote them.

                    Sing the lost, who never
Found, but kept high heart to steer
Onward toward the mark they meant,
Sailing out of sight of land.
Wail not them, nor lost endeavour,
For they heard what tranced the ear,
Filled the exulting soul, the song
Pale and prudent mortals fear,
Song of those who, out of Time,
Sing the heights the immortals climb,
The Sirens.

John Masefield
1874–

THE SHIP

The Ore

BEFORE Man's labouring wisdom gave me birth
I had not even seen the light of day;
Down in the central darkness of the earth,
Crushed by the weight of continents I lay,
Ground by the weight to heat, not knowing then
The air, the light, the noise, the world of men.

The Trees

We grew on mountains where the glaciers cry,
Infinite sombre armies of us stood
Below the snow-peaks which defy the sky;

A song like the gods moaning filled our wood;
We knew no men; our life was to stand stanch,
Singing our song, against the avalanche.

The Hemp and Flax

We were a million grasses on the hill,
A million herbs which bowed as the wind blew,
Trembling in every fibre, never still;
Out of the summer earth sweet life we drew.
Little blue-flowered grasses up the glen,
Glad of the sun, what did we know of men?

The Workers

We tore the iron from the mountain's hold,
By blasting fires we smithied it to steel;
Out of the shapeless stone we learned to mould
The sweeping bow, the rectilinear keel;
We hewed the pine to plank, we split the fir,
We pulled the myriad flax to fashion her.

Out of a million lives our knowledge came,
A million subtle craftsmen forged the means;
Steam was our handmaid, and our servant flame,
Water our strength, all bowed to our machines.
Out of the rock, the tree, the springing herb,
We built this wandering beauty so superb.

The Sailors

We, who were born on earth and live by air,
Make this thing pass across the fatal floor,
The speechless sea; alone we commune there,
Jesting with Death, that ever-open door.
Sun, moon, and stars are signs by which we drive
This wind-blown iron like a thing alive.

The Ship

I march across great waters like a queen,
I whom so many wisdoms helped to make;
Over the uncruddled billows of seas green
I blanch the bubbled highway of my wake.
By me my wandering tenants clasp the hands
And know the thoughts of men in other lands.

Edward Thomas
1878–1917

THE TRUMPET

RISE up, rise up,
   And, as the trumpet blowing
Chases the dreams of men,
As the dawn glowing
The stars that left unlit
The land and water,
Rise up and scatter
The dew that covers
The print of last night's lovers—
Scatter it, scatter it!

While you are listening
To the clear horn,
Forget, men, everything
On this earth new-born,
Except that it is lovelier
Than any mysteries.
Open your eyes to the air
That has washed the eyes of the stars
Through all the dewy night:
Up with the light,
To the old wars:
Arise, arise!

Vachel Lindsay
1879–1931

THE SANTA FÉ TRAIL
(*A Humoresque*)

(I asked the old negro: "What is that bird that sings so well?" He answered: "That is the Rachel-Jane." "Hasn't it another name—lark, or thrush, or the like?" "No. Jus' Rachel-Jane.")

I. IN WHICH A RACING AUTO COMES FROM THE EAST

THIS is the order of the music of the morn-
    ing:—
First, from the far East comes but a crooning.
The crooning turns to a sunrise singing.
Hark to the *calm*-horn, *balm*-horn, *psalm*-horn   *To be sung*
Hark to the *faint*-horn, *quaint*-horn, *saint*-   *delicately, to*
    horn. . . .   *an improvised*
        tune

Hark to the *pace*-horn, *chase*-horn, *race*-horn.   *To be sung or*
And the holy veil of the dawn has gone.   *read with great*
Swiftly the brazen car comes on.   *speed*
It burns in the East as the sunrise burns.
I see great flashes where the far trail turns.
Its eyes are lamps like the eyes of dragons.
It drinks gasoline from big red flagons.
Butting through the delicate mists of the morn-
    ing,
It comes like lightning, goes past roaring.
It will hail all the windmills, taunting, ringing,
Dodge the cyclones,
Count the milestones,
On through the ranges the prairie-dog tills—
Scooting past the cattle on the thousand hills . . .

242

Ho for the tear-horn, scare-horn, dare-horn,
Ho for the *gay*-horn, *bark*-horn, *bay*-horn.
Ho for Kansas, land that restores us
When houses choke us, and great books bore us!
Sunrise Kansas, harvesters' Kansas,
A million men have found you before us.
A million men have found you before us.

To be read or sung in a rolling bass, with some deliberation

II. IN WHICH MANY AUTOS PASS WESTWARD

I want live things in their pride to remain.
I will not kill one grasshopper vain
Though he eats a hole in my shirt like a door.
I let him out, give him one chance more.
Perhaps, when he gnaws my hat in his whim,
Grasshopper lyrics occur to him.

In an even, deliberate, narrative manner

I am a tramp by the long trail's border,
Given to squalor, rags and disorder.
I nap and amble and yawn and look,
Write fool-thoughts in my grubby book,
Recite to the children, explore at my ease,
Work when I work, beg when I please,
Give crank-drawings, that make folks stare
To the half-grown boys in the sunset glare,
And get me a place to sleep in the hay
At the end of a live-and-let-live day.

I find in the stubble of the new-cut weeds
A whisper and a feasting, all one needs:
The whisper of the strawberries, white and red
Here where the new-cut weeds lie dead.

But I would not walk all alone till I die
Without some life-drunk horns going by.
And up round this apple-earth they come
Blasting the whispers of the morning dumb:—

243

Cars in a plain realistic row.
And fair dreams fade
When the raw horns blow.

On each snapping pennant
A big black name:—
The careering city
Whence each car came.
They tour from Memphis, Atlanta, Savannah,
Tallahassee and Texarkana.
They tour from St Louis, Columbus, Manistee,
They tour from Peoria, Davenport, Kankakee.
Cars from Concord, Niagara, Boston,
Cars from Topeka, Emporia, and Austin.
Cars from Chicago, Hannibal, Cairo.
Cars from Alton, Oswego, Toledo.
Cars from Buffalo, Kokomo, Delphi,
Cars from Lodi, Carmi, Loami.
Ho for Kansas, land that restores us
When houses choke us, and great books bore us!

Like a train-caller in a Union Depot

While I watch the highroad
And look at the sky,
While I watch the clouds in amazing grandeur
Roll their legions without rain
Over the blistering Kansas plain—
While I sit by the milestone
And watch the sky,
The United States
Goes by.

Listen to the iron-horns, ripping, racking.
Listen to the quack-horns, slack and clacking.
Way down the road, trilling like a toad,

244

Here comes the *dice*-horn, here comes the *vice*-
    horn,
Here comes the *snarl*-horn, *brawl*-horn, *lewd*-
    horn,
Followed by the *prude*-horn, bleak and squeak-
    ing:—
(Some of them from Kansas, some of them from
    Kansas.)
Here comes the *hod*-horn, *plod*-horn, *sod*-horn,
Nevermore-to-*roam*-horn, *loam*-horn, *home*-
    horn.
(Some of them from Kansas, some of them from
    Kansas.)

*To be given very
harshly, with a
snapping
explosiveness*

  Far away the Rachel-Jane
  Not defeated by the horns
  Sings amid a hedge of thorns:—
  'Love and life,
  Eternal youth—
  Sweet, sweet, sweet, sweet,
  Dew and glory,
  Love and truth,
  Sweet, sweet, sweet, sweet "

*To be read or
sung, well-nigh
in a whisper*

WHILE SMOKE-BLACK FREIGHTS ON THE DOUBLE-
    TRACKED RAILROAD,
DRIVEN AS THOUGH BY THE FOUL FIEND'S OX-
    GOAD,
SCREAMING TO THE WEST COAST, SCREAMING TO
    THE EAST,
CARRY OFF A HARVEST, BRING BACK A FEAST,
AND HARVESTING MACHINERY AND HARNESS FOR
    THE BEAST,
THE HAND-CARS WHIZ, AND RATTLE ON THE
    RAILS,
THE SUNLIGHT FLASHES ON THE TIN DINNER-
    PAILS.

*Louder and
louder, faster
and faster*

And then, in an instant, ye modern men,
Behold the procession once again,
The United States goes by!
Listen to the iron-horns, ripping, racking,
Listen to the *wise*-horn, desperate-to-*advise*
    horn,
Listen to the *fast*-horn, *kill*-horn, *blast*-horn . . .
    Far away the Rachel-Jane
    Not defeated by the horns
    Sings amid a hedge of thorns:—
    Love and life,
    Eternal youth,
    Sweet, sweet, sweet, sweet,
    Dew and glory,
    Love and truth.
    Sweet, sweet, sweet, sweet.
The mufflers open on a score of cars
With wonderful thunder,
CRACK, CRACK, CRACK,
CRACK-CRACK, CRACK-CRACK,
CRACK, CRACK, CRACK,
Listen to the gold-horn . . .
Old-horn . . .
Cold-horn . . .
And all of the tunes, till the night comes down
On hay-stack, and ant-hill, and wind-bitten town.
Then far in the west, as in the beginning,
Dim in the distance, sweet in retreating,
Hark to the faint-horn, quaint-horn, saint-horn,
Hark to the calm-horn, balm-horn, psalm-
    horn . . .

They are hunting the goals that they under-
    stand:—
San-Francisco and the brown sea-sand.

In a rolling bass, with increasing deliberation

With a snapping explosiveness

To be sung or read well-nigh in a whisper

To be brawled in the beginning with a snapping explosiveness, ending in a languorous chant.

To be sung to exactly the same whispered tune as the first five lines

This section beginning sonorously, ending in a languorous whisper

My goal is the mystery the beggars win.
I am caught in the web the night-winds spin.
The edge of the wheat-ridge speaks to me.
I talk with the leaves of the mulberry tree.
And now I hear, as I sit all alone
In the dusk. By another big Santa-Fé stone,
The souls of the tall corn gathering round
And the gay little souls of the grass in the
    ground.
Listen to the tale the cottonwood tells.
Listen to the windmills, singing o'er the wells.
Listen to the whistling flutes without price
Of myriad prophets out of paradise.
Harken to the wonder
That the night-air carries. . . .
Listen . . . to . . . the . . . whisper . .
Of . . . the . . . prairie . . . fairies
Singing o'er the fairy plain:—
"Sweet, sweet, sweet, sweet.
Love and glory,
Stars and rain,
Sweet, sweet, sweet, sweet. . . ."

To the same whispered tune as the Rachel-Jane song—but very slowly

Lascelles Abercrombie

1881–1938

HYMN TO LOVE

WE are thine, O Love, being in thee and made of thee,
    As thóu, Lóve, were the déep thóught
And we the speech of the thought; yea, spoken are we,
    Thy fires of thought out-spoken:

But burn'd not through us thy imagining
    Like fiérce móod in a sóng cáught,
We were as clamour'd words a fool may fling,
    Loose words, of meaning broken.

For what more like the brainless speech of a fool,—
    The lives travelling dark fears,
And as a boy throws pebbles in a pool
    Thrown down abysmal places?

Hazardous are the stars, yet is our birth
    And our journeying time theirs;
As words of air, life makes of starry earth
    Sweet soul-delighted faces;

As voices are we in the worldly wind;
    The great wind of the world's fate
Is turned, as air to a shapen sound, to mind
    And marvellous desires.

But not in the world as voices storm-shatter'd,
    Not borne down by the wind's weight;
The rushing time rings·with our splendid word
    Like darkness filled with fires.

For Love doth use us for the sound of song,
    And Love's meaning our life wields,
Making our souls like syllables to throng
    His tunes of exultation.

Down the blind speed of a fatal world we fly,
    As rain blown along earth's fields;
Yet are we god-desiring liturgy,
    Sung songs of adoration;

Yea, made of chance and all a labouring strife,
    We go charged with a strong flame;
For as a language Love hath seized on life
    His burning heart to story.

Yea, Love, we are thine, the liturgy of thee,
    Thy thought's golden and glad name,
The mortal conscience of immortal glee,
    Love's zeal in Love's own glory.

from EMBLEMS OF LOVE

Rupert Brooke

1887-1915

THE SONG OF THE PILGRIMS

(Halted around the fire by night, after moon-set,
they sing this beneath the trees)

WHAT light of unremembered skies
        Hast thou relumed within our eyes,
Thou whom we seek, whom we shall find? . . .
A certain odour on the wind,
Thy hidden face beyond the west,
These things have called us; on a quest
Older than any road we trod,
More endless than desire. . . .
                            Far God,
Sigh with thy cruel voice, that fills
The soul with longing for dim hills
And faint horizons! For there come
Grey moments of the antient dumb
Sickness of travel, when no song
Can cheer us; but the way seems long;

And one remembers. . . .

                        Ah! the beat
Of weary unreturning feet,
And songs of pilgrims unreturning! . . .
The fires we left are always burning
On the old shrines of home. Our kin
Have built them temples, and therein
Pray to the Gods we know; and dwell
In little houses lovable,
Being happy (we remember how!)
And peaceful even to death. . . .

                          O Thou,
God of all long desirous roaming,
Our hearts are sick of fruitless homing,
And crying after lost desire.
Hearten us onward! as with fire
Consuming dreams of other bliss.
The best Thou givest, giving this
Sufficient thing—to travel still
Over the plain, beyond the hill,
Unhesitating through the shade,
Amid the silence unafraid,
Till, at some sudden turn, one sees
Against the black and muttering trees
Thine altar, wonderfully white,
Among the Forests of the Night.